THE PATRICK PEARSE MOTEL

A Comedy

HUGH LEONARD

ench's
ting
tion

D1502603

THE
PATRICK PEARSE
MOTEL

A Comedy

by

HUGH LEONARD

SAMUEL   FRENCH

LONDON
NEW YORK TORONTO SYDNEY HOLLYWOOD

© 1971 BY HUGH LEONARD

PRINTED IN GREAT BRITAIN
This impression printed by photolithography from the original printing
by W & J Mackay Limited, Chatham

THE PATRICK PEARSE MOTEL

First presented at the Dublin Theatre Festival on
15th March 1971 at the Olympia Theatre, Dublin,
with the following cast:

Dermod Gibbon	Frank Kelly
Grainne Gibbon	Rosaleen Linehan
Fintan Kinnore	Godfrey Quigley
Niamh Kinnore	May Cluskey
James Usheen	John Gregson
Miss Manning	Angela Vale
Hoolihan	Derry Power

Director: James Grout
Designer: Patrick Murray

Later presented by H. M. Tennent at the Queen's
Theatre, London, with the following cast

Dermod Gibbon	Patrick Laffan
Grainne Gibbon	Moira Redmond
Fintan Kinnore	Godfrey Quigley
Niamh Kinnore	May Cluskey
James Usheen	Norman Rodway
Miss Manning	Rosemary Martin
Hoolihan	Derry Power

The play directed by James Grout
Settings by Patrick Murray

ACT I

The living-room of Dermod and Grainne Gibbon
in Foxrock—a suburb in Dublin's vodka-and-
bitter-lemon belt. A winter's evening

ACT II

Scene 1 The Motel. Fifteen minutes later
Scene 2 The same. A few minutes later

Time - the present

NOTE–pronunciation–Niamh is pronounced 'Neeve
Grainne is pronounced '*Graw*-nyeh'

ACT I

The living-room of Dermod and Grainne. A winter's evening

The room is an object lesson in gracious living. The rugs match the window-curtains and the curtains harmonize with the covers and cushions. The coffee-table is marble. There is a mini-chandelier. On the walls are a Yeats, a Keating and an O'Sullivan. A handsome antique cabinet houses the most expensive hi-fi system in Foxrock; huge loud-speakers stand at opposite ends of the room. There are two doors: one leads to the hall, the other into a small bar with stools. The bar is a recent conversion: it is under the stairs, so that the ceiling slopes down sharply, the result being that no-one who is more than five foot two inches in height can stand erect in it

For ten seconds before the Curtain rises we hear the amplified sound of a game of ping-pong in progress. When the Curtain rises, Dermod, Grainne, Niamh and her husband Fintan Kinnore are seated on the floor with their backs to the audience. They are listening to a stereo demonstration disc. The ping-pong ball seems to travel from one end of the room to the other. They turn their heads in perfect unison as if at a tennis match. The track comes to an end, and an American voice is heard from one of the speakers

Compère Anyone for ping—(*from the other speaker*)—pong?
Fintan (*getting up*) What'll they think of next?
Dermod No, stay there—there's more.
Grainne Isn't stereo wonderful—we're thinking of buying another record.
Dermod Sssh! This is fantastic. Can you guess what this is?
Niamh Is it someone throwing up?
Dermod It's sea-lions.
Fintan Certainly it's sea-lions. (*To the others*) She hears them every day!

The recording ends. Dermod rises and switches off the power. The others get to their feet

A quick look at them. Dermod and Grainne are youngish and attractive. He is thirty-five or so, watches his weight, is go-ahead, wears horn-rims, which give him a deceptively earnest look. His clothes are well-cut; he wears a "dress" sweater and an ornate medallion. Grainne is petite. Her friendliness and beauty attract men; her poise and faintly goddess-like air tend to keep them at their distance. She speaks well. She and Dermod might have been born for affluent living; there is no trace of the parvenu about either of them. They hold hands and hug each other a great deal—always a dangerous sign. Fintan and Niamh are older: God knows they try hard, but prosperity sits on them both like a donkey on a thistle. Fintan is big, suspicious, inflammable. Niamh is the kind of woman on whom an expensive piece of haute couture would resemble a canvas awning. She does her best, but even her walk suggests a dignified gallop.

Niamh That was beautiful, Dermod.
Fintan Highly impressive.
Dermod (*modestly*) It's not bad.
Niamh I love the gramophone.
Fintan How much did it run you?
Dermod Five-seven-five.
Fintan That's not bad.
Dermod What about this, though? (*He operates another switch*)

Fintan and Niamh listen intently. Utter silence

Fintan (*impressed*) Will you listen to that!

Niamh looks at him, decides that she is in the wrong place, moves down and sits on the floor

Oh, leave it to the Japs.
Dermod It's on in the master bedroom.
Fintan (*who is nobody's fool*) Oh, I knew it was somewhere. (*He notices Niamh. In an embarrassed whisper*) Get up.
Dermod (*operating another switch*) Now it's on in the sauna.
Fintan By God, what?
Niamh (*on her hands and knees*) Such things as they invent. It's a great improvement on the old horny gramophones.

Fintan looks at her

Graine, do you remember the old horny gramophones?
Grainne No.
Fintan Will you get up!
Niamh Why, is it off?
Dermod Yes.
Fintan Yes!

Niamh gets to her feet

Dermod Who's for a drink?
Fintan (*looking at his watch*) Ummm . . .
Grainne Shouldn't you and Mr Kinnore be off soon?
Fintan ⎫
Niamh ⎭ Fintan, Fintan!
Grainne Fintan. Shouldn't you?
Dermod No rush. If we leave at nine we'll still be in Cork by midnight.
Grainne (*with a hint of alarm*) Nine? You said you were leaving at eight-thirty.
Dermod (*shrugging*) Give or take. (*Putting his arms round her*) She can't wait to be rid of me.
Grainne (*playing his game*) You're right.
Dermod Got a boy-friend in the loft, haven't you?
Grainne (*shaking her head*) In the hot press.

Dermod (*nuzzling her*) Hope he smothers.

Niamh (*watching their display of affection*) It's like an advertisement for glue.

Fintan, who is easily moved to passion, strokes her bottom

Stop that.

Fintan Some people might do well to show a quarter as much affection.

Niamh If you mean me, I don't have to. You've got enough in you for an orgy.

Grainne (*to Dermod*) Love, I hate to think of you drinking and then driving all that distance.

Dermod We'll be careful.

Grainne And the weather is so awful.

Fintan Is it still raining?

Niamh I'll see. (*She walks with dignity to the window, pulls the curtain aside and looks out*)

Fintan Well?

Niamh It's urinating.

Grainne There!

Niamh (*to Fintan, who is glaring at her*) You told me not to use the other word.

Dermod We have time for just the one. If you'll all step into the consulting room . . . !

They all go into the bar. The height of the ceiling obliges them to remain half-crouching while they are there. Dermod goes behind the bar and begins to open a bottle of champagne

Grainne Wouldn't we be more comfortable in the living-room?

Dermod What's the point of having a bar put in if we don't drink in it?

Niamh Oh, this is very snug.

Dermod It's not bad, is it?

Fintan How much?

Dermod Twelve-fifty, with fittings.

Niamh It's so original. I love sunken ceilings.

Grainne Believe it or not, that part of it was accidental.

Niamh Go 'way!

Dermod Absolutely.

Fintan By God.

Niamh begins to climb up on a bar stool, facing it as if it were a ladder. She is trying to avoid hitting her head

Grainne (*pointing upwards*) It's the stairs, you see. We thought of having them raised slightly, but . . .

Niamh Don't do that, you'll spoil it. (*She tries to turn into a sitting position on the stool*)

Fintan (*taking hold of her by the thighs*) Do you want a hand?

Niamh (*a mite tetchy*) I'm all right, I'm all right. (*To Grainne*) Don't touch it, it's perfect.

*A "pop" is heard from behind the bar as Dermod uncorks the champagne.
The bottle comes into sight. Niamh sees it*

Oh, Jay, looka . . .

Fintan glares at her

Champagne—how lovely.

Dermod Well, it's an occasion. Fintan, here's to a long partnership and a successful day in Cork.

Grainne And prosperity.

Dermod Same thing, love.

Fintan No, here's to friendship—friends through and through, and to hell with money. (*He drinks*) Good stuff. How much?

Dermod Ten-ten a half-doz.

Fintan That's with discount?

Dermod Sure.

Fintan I'll buy a gross.

Grainne Darling, must you go to Cork?

Dermod (*fondly*) Now, now . . .

Grainne Don't. Stay home with me.

Dermod Can't.

Grainne Yes!

Fintan (*tolerantly*) Women, women! I'll have him back to you this time tomorrow night, with the deeds to a brand new motel.

Dermod What'll we call this one?

Fintan It's in Cork. Who's the most famous patriot from there?

Dermod Michael Collins.

Fintan The "Michael Collins"!

Niamh Gorgeous.

Dermod (*refilling Fintan's glass*) Fintan, you're a genius.

Fintan (*crowing*) Our second motel—and the first one not even open yet!

Dermod Only one week to go!

Grainne Stay here tonight.

Dermod I can't. We . . .

Grainne I'll be all on my own.

Dermod No, you won't, you'll be staying with Niamh.

Grainne It's not the same thing. I want to be *here*, with you.

Dermod Fintan, tell her . . .

Grainne I don't care. You're mean. Where are my cigarettes?

*Grainne goes into the living-room. Her peevishness at once disappears. She
makes a dive for her handbag, fishes out her spectacles and peers myoptically
at her wristwatch*

Fintan By God, that girl is mad about you.

Niamh Can't bear to let him out of her sight.

Dermod (*modestly*) I know, I know.

Niamh Lovebirds!

Grainne (*with a howl of anguish*) Half-past eight—is the rotten pig going to stay here all night? (*Hissing towards the bar*) Get out, get out, go to Cork, go to Cork! Oh God, will you make the stupid, useless maggot go to C . . . (*She breaks off, suddenly noticing the presence of us, the audience. She holds her glasses to her eyes, just to make sure, then hastily puts them back in her handbag. She smiles at us charmingly, now the perfect hostess*) Welcome, welcome to our home. I do wish you could see all of it. You'd adore my kitchen: it's eighteenth-century English and all-electric. And the master bedroom is a dream: in white, everything built-in, and the carpet so deep, if you lost an ear-ring you'd need a safari to find it. (*She laughs at her little joke*) And there's a sunken bath —Dermod got the idea from *Spartacus*—all done in tiles inspired by the graffiti at Pompeii: daring, but nice. And I can just see you all sitting in our sauna. (*She looks at us for a moment, imagining this. Then, anxious for our good opinion*) I hope I don't seem to boast? Dermod and I couldn't always afford little extras. But he worked so hard—well, I won't bore you, but we were in this teeny flat, and there was this government contract, because the Department of Defence had sold their aeroplane. *You know*—the jet. But they shouldn't have, because the Department of Agriculture had nothing to spray crops with. A-a-nnnd, they wanted it back, and there was this purchasing contract. A-a-nnnd there was this man who seemed certain to get it, only some awful person reported him for diddling the income tax, so he didn't get it; and it turned out that the poor man hadn't been—diddling, I mean, but by then Dermod had the contract, and that was the beginning. And now we have all this, and we're so happy and grateful and sincerely humble. Because we're still simple people who sit home and look at colour television, just like you do. *Some* things are different: we swopped our old parish priest for a Jesuit; and *he* told us that the bit about the rich man and the camel going through the eye of a needle doesn't apply in areas where poverty has been eradicated—such as Foxrock. Does money bring happiness? Well, I have my ring and my brooch (*showing them*) and nice clothes— you'll see my coat later—and my car, and, of course, Dermod; and I can assure you—(*her voice quavers as she descends further into abject misery with each word*)—that I'm the most—content and the happiest—girl in the whole—wide—world. (*She dissolves into tears and gropes for her handkerchief*)

Dermod comes from the bar. He heads for the telephone and dials a number

(*Coldly*) Who are you phoning?
Dermod (*his joke*) My girl-friend.
Grainne (*with a snort of derision*) Huh!
Dermod No, that's one thing that'll never come between us, love. You'll always be the only girl for me. (*He blows her a kiss*)

Grainne blows him a kiss back, then turns away

Grainne (*in utter disgust*) Yeccch!
Dermod Fintan reminded me that our new manageress is due in town. I

don't want her ringing here and getting no answer, with us in Cork and you staying with Niamh. (*Into the phone*) Come on, come on . . .

Niamh (*in the bar*) Fintan, help me down, I'm getting a nose-bleed.

Fintan helps her down

And will you stop feeling me—you've been at it all night.

Fintan I can't help it.

Niamh Yes, you can.

Fintan You're so lovely.

Niamh You must be as blind as a bat.

Fintan Fifteen years, and every time I look at you I go mad inside. I don't know what I'm going to do in Cork without you.

Niamh I know what I'm going to do tonight—sleep! Oh, just to lie in an empty bed, to be able to roll over without a voice roaring in me ear, "Good girl, good girl, here I am!"

Fintan (*sure of himself*) Not at all: you'll cry yourself to sleep without me. Ah, don't fret, girl, I'll make it up to you tomorrow night on the double.

Niamh (*hollowly*) Oh, God!

Dermod (*into the telephone*) Hello, Royal Shamrock Hotel? . . . You might answer your switchboard—do you call this efficiency? . . . I want no lip, thank you. Has Miss Manning checked in yet? . . . Yes, she is: I myself made the reservation . . . But she must be; she was due at six from London . . . You did what? . . . That was damned officious of you . . . Oh, yes? Well, will you kindly tell your manager he'll be hearing from me. The name is Gibbon. Dermod Gibbon of Mother Ireland Motels, Limited. (*He hangs up*) Bloody nerve.

Grainne What is?

Dermod She hasn't turned up, so they've cancelled her room.

Grainne So?

Dermod (*angrily*) I made that reservation.

Grainne (*feigning horror*) And they cancelled it? Oh, the fools.

Dermod Not funny, love. I'll ring the airport.

Grainne (*agitated*) You haven't time. I'll do it. You go to Cork.

Dermod (*mildly amused*) Haven't time? What's the matter with you? (*He dials. Through the following he gets his number and talks into the phone*)

Niamh (*in the bar*) I'll tell you what's the matter with you. You're so randy that you can't even look at a wasp without imagining it with its stripes off.

Fintan "Randy"—that's exquisite language from a woman's mouth.

Niamh And what's more, you're twisted.

Fintan Me?

Niamh Anyone who likes ugly women *must* be twisted.

Fintan What ugly woman? (*Pointing out of the bar*) Do you mean her? That ugly article out there?

Grainne, who looks anything but an "ugly article", idly smoothes her dress over her thighs, her head thrown back: the effect is definitely erotic

Sure a man would be mad to look at her twice!

Niamh (*half to herself*) It's true, I knew it—he's woman-blind.

Fintan I know what your game is; you're trying to get me confused. There's another man.

Niamh (*stunned*) A what?

Fintan I'm not enough for you. You want to use that body of yours to to drag other poor unfortunates to their destruction.

Niamh What body?

Fintan And that face. Beside you, Cleopatra was an oul' ratbag.

Niamh stares towards the audience, her face numb with stupefaction

Well, you're not going to get the chance to exercise your lust while I'm in Cork. That ugly article out there is going to stay with you—that was *my* idea. And if I ever catch you looking crossways at a man I'll crucify you and I'll tear him to bits. Do you hear me?

Niamh (*frightened by his towering rage*) Yes, Fintan.

Dermod (*on the telephone*) Closed down completely? Nothing getting off at all?

Niamh, drink in hand, makes to move out of the bar

Fintan Come back here. You mind your manners, because that bugger is putting me up for the country club, and men of substance who get into the country club do not have wives who at the first sight of a bottle of champagne say, "Ah, jay—looka!"

Niamh You're always telling me to be myself.

Fintan At home—not when you're out. Go on, now.

Niamh and Fintan move out of the bar as Dermod hangs up

Niamh (*emerging at a half-stoop*) We thought we'd come out before we were left this way.

Fintan (*glaring at her; to Dermod*) What's the news of your Miss Manning?

Grainne (*to Niamh, in an urgent whisper*) I've got to talk to you.

Dermod London Airport is closed for the night. Fog.

Fintan Well, there's no rush, she'll ... (*Seeing that Niamh has not straightened up*) You're out now, pet. (*To Dermod*) She'll be here tomorrow.

Dermod I promise you, she's a jewel. I met her at a cocktail party in London. Grainne's old boy-friend was there—James Usheen.

Niamh (*excitedly*) Oh, you don't mean the one on television? (*To Grainne*) You don't know *him*?

Grainne (*with a tight smile*) I used to.

Dermod Before he was famous. Her first love, yes?

Grainne Something like that.

Niamh You and him? Oh, Jay—mes Usheen, how interesting for you.

Grainne (*wishing the subject had not come up*) It was twelve years ago. I haven't seen him since—except on the box.

Niamh I watch him every Sunday. I love him when he's insulting people.

Fintan Is he in colour?

Niamh Yes.

Fintan I'd have seen him, so.

Niamh He's here now.

Grainne (*whirling round, her hand on her throat*) Where?

Niamh Here in town. He's opening a supermarket. I saw it in the *News of the World* . . .

Fintan looks at her

. . . *The Times*. Do you remember how he got famous? When he made that remark on the television—"Homosexuality is only a pain in the a . . ."

Fintan That'll do!

Niamh I'm only saying what he . . .

Fintan Well, don't—(*for the benefit of the others*)—pet. Yes, I know him now. Didn't some husband get costs off him in a divorce case? And he's on every Sunday, belittling his own country and running down the sacrament of marriage. Oh, a credit to us—if he was in black-and-white I'd switch him off.

Grainne They say he's a horrid person; let's not talk about him. (*Feigning surprise*) Look at the time! Where does the evening go to? Now—coats!

Grainne goes out, humming to herself and trying not to hurry

Fintan You've got a fine girl there.

Dermod I know.

Fintan She's a monument to your good taste. Not many men appreciate that beneath a plain exterior there often beats a heart of gold.

Dermod (*at sea*) Pardon?

Niamh (*softly*) You can take him nowhere.

Fintan It was a very beautiful woman that first said that to me. Did you ever meet my ex-secretary, Miss Shanahan? Oh, a smasher. She was the spitting image of Robert Morley.

Dermod Is that so?

Fintan She went into a convent.

Niamh I wonder why.

Fintan A shocking waste. (*Business-like*) Partner, I'll be honest with you. There are women and women—man-eaters like this one—(*indicating Niamh*)—and decent plain creatures like your wife. But I don't like the sound of this new manageress of yours.

Dermod Miss Manning?

Grainne returns, carrying overcoats and scarves

Grainne Here we are. Now both of you wrap up well.

Dermod Because she was at a cocktail party? Fintan, she is the dowdiest, dullest, most . . .

Fintan I accept that.

Dermod Then why?

Grainne Let me help you.

Grainne helps the men into their coats and scarves. They are too involved in their argument to notice. Niamh looks at her empty glass and goes into the bar for a refill

Dermod If it's her qualifications . . .
Fintan No, it's her nationality.
Dermod (*disbelieving*) Because she's English? Oh, Fintan . . . !
Fintan Don't misunderstand me: I'm not a bigot. Ordinarily I wouldn't care if she was a black. (*On second thoughts*) Well, if she was a—Norwegian.
Dermod But . . .
Fintan We decided, you and I did, to run our motels on patriotic principles as a tribute to the men who died for Ireland. We owe it to them.
Dermod Absolutely. (*To Grainne*) Thanks, love. But I don't see . . .
Fintan Next week, five miles up those mountains—(*he points out*)—we'll have our first grand opening. The motel will be named after the greatest patriot of all time. The Tricolor and the Plough and the Stars will float over the swimming-pool, there will be an oil painting of a different patriot in every bedroom. Look—look at the menu. (*He produces a sheet of paper*) "Battle of the Boyne Salmon—Vinegar Hill Mayonnaise—Black and Tan Pigs' Feet—I.R.A. Bombe Surprise . . ."
Dermod Yes, and "Remember Limerick Ham". But what has that to . . .
Fintan It has this to do with it. With all the patriotism I wouldn't feel right having a manageress who was English.
Dermod I disagree. (*To Grainne, absently*) Thanks, dear. (*To Fintan*) I think we've more than done our bit. There's a night-watchmen out there now who served in the nineteen-sixteen rising. He's too old to be efficient but we hired him. We advertised for a manageress, and you saw the applicants. Any one of them would have ruined us in a month. Ireland first, Fintan, and at all costs. But it is not patriotic to lose money. It is a betrayal of the economy.
Fintan My answer is still no.
Dermod Miss Manning has a contract. She could sue us.
Fintan Let her.
Dermod And she'll win.
Fintan (*after a pause*) I am a patriot. But I don't want to look like a fanatic —we'll give her a try.
Dermod Fintan, you have greatness in you.
Grainne There—you're weather-proof! (*She kisses Dermod*) Good-bye, my darling. Think of me and drive carefully. I'll miss you.
Fintan But I'd like to see her references.
Grainne And I wish you every success in Cork.
Dermod They're upstairs in my workroom. I'll get them.
Fintan I'll go with you. I need to use the amenities.

Dermod and Fintan go out. Grainne has been too intent on getting rid of them to pay heed to what has been said

Grainne (*calling musically*) Niamh, Fintan is go-ing! (*It dawns on her that they have merely gone upstairs*) Dermod, Cork is *that* way! Oh, my God.

Niamh comes out of the bar

(*Ashen-faced*) They're still here.

Niamh I know. Before Fintan goes anywhere he always mauls me good-bye.

Grainne (*shoving her wristwatch under Niamh's nose*) What time is it?

Niamh Quarter to.

Grainne I'm done for. They're going to stay on and on, and when he comes they'll still be here.

Niamh When who comes?

Grainne Who? Who? Who do you think? James Usheen!

Niamh *Him?*

Grainne Yes!

Niamh Shaggin' hell.

Grainne Have you got the letter?

Niamh What?

Grainne The *letter!*

Niamh (*in a daze*) It came yesterday. (*She takes an envelope from her handbag and glances at the printed heading*) The Royal Anna Liffey Hotel.

Grainne That's the one.

Niamh He's—coming here?

Grainne He's due now.

Niamh And Dermod doesn't . . .

Grainne Sssh! No.

Niamh Will I see him?

Grainne You'll do much more than see him. I need your help.

Niamh What for—to jump on him? (*She laughs*)

Grainne (*grimly*) If there's any jumping to be done, I'll do it.

Niamh gapes at her, realizing she is in earnest.

If only they'd go to Cork! Niamh, do you know what it's like, living in England? Over there women have affairs.

Niamh Do they?

Grainne For God's sake, love, don't you read your *Nova?* They have freedom. In a big city a woman is like a needle with a haystack to hide in, and she's never caught.

Niamh Some are.

Grainne Not so many. The *News of the World* never goes more than thirty-two pages.

Niamh (*nodding*) And eight of those are sport.

Grainne I have never looked at any man except Dermod. Where's the point? A man can take one look at a woman and love her for the rest of his life. But we women are different. We're realists.

Niamh I know. Just looking at a steak won't fill your stomach.

Grainne You expressed that very well, Niamh.

Niamh Ta.

Grainne I've tried to be a wife, not a vegetable. I take guitar lessons, I've studied Irish art, and I read Harold Robbins. In this country women are bond-slaves. I love Ireland. I believe that whatever English women have, we owe it to our pride as a nation to let Irish women have some of it, too.

Niamh There's an awful lot of patriotism around here this evening.

Grainne God has given me so very much. But it's the little things we can't have that turn us into monsters. I want to spare Dermod that, Niamh.

Niamh (*touched*) Aren't you good to him!

Grainne (*with sudden passion*) Apart from which, he is so bloody dull, and this house is dull, and I would love to have a man just once, just once before my throat gets wrinkles and people look at my brooch first and my ring, and then me, and I swear, I swear I will never ask for another thing so long as I live—just one short fleeting night of harmless innocent adultery. Oh, God, is that too much to ask for?

Niamh (*after a pause*) Have you tried St Ann?

Grainne (*calmly*) I had almost given up hope, then Dermod met James Usheen at the party. He introduced himself as my husband. Next day, James rang me. He said he was coming over to open a supermarket, and could we meet? He sounded so affectionate.

Niamh (*half horror, half awe*) You wouldn't!

Grainne When Dermod said that he and Fintan were going to Cork this evening, I knew it was a sign from heaven. I booked a double room in your name at the Royal Anna Liffey Hotel. (*Hugging the letter*) That's why I had them send you the confirmation.

Niamh In my name?

Grainne Yours and Fintan's.

Niamh He'll slaughter me.

Grainne He won't know. I've planned every little detail, and if only they'll stop dithering upstairs and go to Cork, then nothing—positively nothing—can go wrong. (*She looks at the letter and emits a shriek of horror*)

Niamh What is it?

Grainne The hotel's full up.

Dermod returns

Niamh Ah, no.

Grainne They can't take us.

Niamh Well, isn't that the . . .

Dermod Who can't take you?

Grainne and Niamh swing around to stare at him. Grainne thrusts the letter behind her back

Grainne The hairdresser.

Niamh (*simultaneously*) The chiropodist.

Dermod Both full up, are they? Hard luck. Say good-bye, love. We're off.

He moves towards Grainne to kiss her good-bye. She backs away, comes up against the table on which is Niamh's handbag and, operating by touch, shoves the letter blindly into it

> *Fintan enters to say his good-bye. Niamh looks apprehensively at him and so does not see what Grainne is doing with the letter*

Dermod Take care, darling. I'll miss you.
Grainne I'll miss you, too. Now be good.
Dermod (*fondly*) *You* be good.
Grainne (*lovingly, groping for the handbag*) What do *you* think?

Fintan advances on Niamh

Niamh Keep away from me.
Fintan I want to say good-bye.
Niamh The only thing worse than you saying good-bye is you saying hello. (*As he closes with her*) Now get off!
Fintan (*to the others, struggling with Niamh*) It's our little game, isn't she great?
Grainne Don't go.
Dermod Must. (*A last kiss*) 'Bye. Fintan . . . ?
Niamh Oh, you messer.
Fintan (*thickly*) Right. (*He manages to plant a kiss on Niamh's face*) Now remember what I said.
Niamh Yes!
Fintan (*as a threat*) And mind yourself—pet. Good-bye, Mrs Gibbon.
Grainne Grainne.
Dermod 'Bye, Niamh.

> *Dermod and Fintan go out. Grainne sees them to the front door, off*

Niamh, exhausted by her battle with Fintan, sags into a chair

Dermod (*off*) Don't come out in the rain, love, 'bye!
Grainne (*off*) Drive carefully!

> *Grainne comes back into the living-room*

Niamh In bed or out of it, he's the same. He comes at me like a threshing machine.
Grainne Sssh! (*She listens*)

Car doors are slammed off. There is the sound of the engine starting up, then the noise of wheels on gravel

> Gone! (*She gives a broad smile*)
Niamh What are you looking so happy about? If the hotel is full up . . .
Grainne There's one other place we can go to.
Niamh At this hour?

Grainne It came to me while I was kissing Dermod good-bye. What does P.P. stand for?

Niamh The parish priest's house? You wouldn't!

Grainne I mean the Patrick Pearse.

Niamh The motel?

Grainne Why not? It's furnished, the heating's on, and there are eighty-four bedrooms, all empty. There's even a swimming-pool, in case James turns out to be kinky.

Niamh But the night watchman . . .

Grainne He doesn't know me by sight; Dermod engaged him. And next week, when the motel is open, he'll be let go, he'll never see me again. It's perfect.

Niamh If men only knew what goes on inside women's heads while they're kissing them! But, Grainne, you can't—not in Dermod's motel.

Grainne In a way, it's appropriate. When a ship is launched it's always the owner's wife who christens it. Now I must go upstairs and change.

Niamh Out of *that* dress?

Grainne For James—nothing but the best. Niamh, be a love and fetch me a drink, I'm shaking with nerves. Oh, when he finds out what I've got in store for him!

Niamh (*stunned*) He doesn't know?

Grainne How could he? Do you take me for the kind of woman who would tell a man she intends to go to bed with him? He'd think I was fast.

Niamh Yeah—I'm sorry.

Grainne (*beginning to unzip her dress*) The drinks, love—and have one yourself.

Again the sound of car wheels on gravel is heard

It's too late, he's here! (*Babbling*) I left the door off the catch, I told him to come straight in. One never looks one's best on a doorstep. Niamh, I want the first thing he sees to be me, alone, waiting, So would you . . . ?

Niamh Would I what?

Grainne (*pointing to the bar*) Please?

Niamh nods, crosses herself resignedly, and goes into the bar. Grainne braces herself for the great moment. As footsteps are heard in the hall, she shuts her eyes dreamily and extends her arms towards the open door, ready to be embraced

Darling——

But it is Fintan who appears

—is it really you?

Fintan No, he's out in the car.

Grainne (*staring at him*) Oh.

Fintan Niamh's Mini is blocking the drive. (*Yelling*) Niamh!

Niamh (*in the bar*) What?

Grainne I was just going upstairs to—pack a suitcase.

Grainne goes out

Niamh (*yelling from the bar*) What do you want?
Fintan Your car is in our way. Where are the keys?
Niamh In my handbag. (*She pours a drink for herself and for Grainne*)

Fintan finds her handbag, rummages inside it, takes out the letter, looks at it, puts it back, finds the key, shuts the handbag, and starts for the door. Half- way across the room he comes to a shuddering stop. He goes racing back to the handbag, takes the letter out again and reads it. Disbelief gives way to a convulsion of sheer, towering rage. He growls like an animal and raises his hands above his head, the letter crushed in his fist. Niamh comes from the bar, a glass of champagne in each hand

(*Coldly*) Why don't you go to Cork—you're not wanted here. And leave my keys in the dashboard.

He reaches for her as if about to strangle her

And don't paw me with my hands full.

Niamh goes out

Fintan sits brokenly and begins to sob

Dermod comes in

Dermod What's the delay for? (*Looking at him*) Why are you laughing?

Fintan holds out the letter. Dermod takes it

What is it? (*He smoothes out the letter and reads it*) So? You and Niamh tried to book into the Royal Anna Liffey tonight and it's full up. What's so . . . (*He looks at the letter again*) Tonight? But . . .

A heartrending sob from Fintan

Fintan, stop that.
Fintan It was—in her handbag.
Dermod Yes?
Fintan Her and some bollix.
Dermod Good God.
Fintan Me in Cork, and her in her element.
Dermod Niamh? I don't believe it.
Fintan (*with a terrible roar*) I'll kill her! (*He lurches towards the door, blind with rage*)
Dermod (*grabbing him*) Fintan, no.
Fintan Let go of me.
Dermod Not until you control yourself. The state you're in, now, you might kill her.

Fintan I will, I will.

Dermod Yes, and then what?

Fintan What do you mean, then what? We'll have it hushed up, what do you think? Now get your hands off.

Dermod Fintan, listen to me. We're going to Cork . . .

Fintan To hell with Cork, I'm not going to Cork, I never liked Cork.

Dermod (*quietly, in charge*) We are going to Cork, because whatever Niamh was up to, it's fallen through. (*Showing Fintan the letter*) The hotel is full up. Furthermore, Grainne will be with her tonight in your house, and there'll be no monkey business with her there. In Cork, you can think things over calmly, and tomorrow you can sort it all out with Niamh in a civilized manner.

Fintan You're right.

Dermod Good man.

Fintan I'll kill her tomorrow.

Dermod Have you her car keys? (*He sees that Fintan is holding the keys and takes them from him*)

Fintan Maybe I ought to kill her now.

Dermod No!

Fintan I didn't get where I am today by putting things off. Can you wait five minutes? (*He makes for the door*)

Dermod Fintan!

Fintan Why did I have to marry a raving beauty? Do you know what I'm going to do? I'll choke her till there's just enough breath left in her gizzard to gasp out the name of the man. And when I find him . . . !

Dermod (*shaking him violently*) Fintan!

Fintan looks glassily at him

Cork.

Fintan (*childlike*) Cork?

Dermod And money.

Fintan Money . . .

Dermod That's the man! (*He leads the suddenly docile Fintan by the hand to the door*)

As they reach the door, Niamh enters, passing them, with her own glass of champagne. Fintan emits a terrible roar and is about to spring at her, but Dermod yanks him out into the hall. By the time Niamh turns around they are both gone.

Niamh (*assuming that the roar was a sneeze*) Bless you. (*Calling*) Grainne, they've——

Grainne enters. She has changed into her newest, most stunning dress, and carries the other glass of champagne

——gone.

Grainne I know, I saw them. Zip me up?

We hear the sound of the car moving off

How do I look?

Niamh In that dress you won't have time to get to the motel. It'll happen in the middle of the road.

Grainne (*coolly*) No, it won't. It's all going to be beautiful.

Niamh But it's a sin.

Grainne laughs

Yes, yes, it is.

Grainne Father Semple, our Jesuit, said to me that if there was no sin there would be no need for priests, and if there were no priests everybody in the country would be committing adultery. Well, if we're going to turn into a race of degenerates it won't be my fault. That's why there's that bit in the Bible about a man laying down his life for his friend. So it's . . .

Niamh No, stop. You've lost me, and if I'm confused I won't sleep—and tonight I am going to sleep. (*Ecstatically*) When I stretch out in that big bed it's going to be like lying in a field, and not a bull in sight.

Grainne You poor thing.

Niamh (*hastily*) I don't want you to think badly of Fintan. He's the kindest man in the world—yes, he is. And it's not even the night after night I object to. You'll think I'm too sensitive, but what I've come to dread, what turns me into a nervous wreck, is waiting for the very last minute, when he roars "Up the rebels!". What the English did to the Irish for seven hundred years Fintan's been doing to me for the past fifteen. How is Dermod that way?

Grainne Nothing.

Niamh Do you mean he doesn't roar?

Grainne I mean nothing, nothing.

Niamh But he's never done hugging you.

Grainne That's for visitors.

Niamh (*nodding*) I *thought* you looked very fresh. But why?

Grainne (*shaking her head*) I'm not a disobliging wife, I know my duty. Every night I lie on my bed with my face smothered in the cream I wear to keep my pores open, just for him. And he sits on *his* bed totting up figures and looking at me as if I were the Man in the Iron Mask.

Niamh Twin beds. Oh, Jay.

Grainne His new Jensen gets more affection than I do. At least *it* gets driven. But when James Usheen walks through that door . . . !

Niamh I don't want to hear. What'll you do?

Grainne Not a thing. He'll take one look and sweep me into his arms.

Niamh Oh, Jay, don't go on.

Grainne Did you read what the judge called him in that divorce case? A dedicated philanderer. And yet, when I knew him, he was all pimples and damp hands. I used to scream whenever he touched me. But *now*, oh, when I look at that man on television! So debonair, so beautifully dressed, and that low-pitched sexy voice!

The door bursts open and James Usheen staggers in. His overcoat and most of his face are caked with mud

Usheen (*croaking*) Where's the fucking brandy?
Grainne ⎫
Niamh ⎬ (*pointing*) In the bar. ⎰ *speaking*
          ⎱ *together*

Without pausing for a moment, Usheen goes into the bar, hitting his head on the ceiling

Usheen Shite!
Grainne James!
Niahm It's him!

They rush into the bar, where Usheen is nursing his head with one hand and pouring himself a drink with the other

Grainne James, what's happened to you? You . . .
Usheen Belt up, will you—I think I may drop dead.

They watch as he knocks back a brandy

That's better. Who owned this house before you did—pygmies?
Graimme James, your clothes . . .
Usheen I'm lucky to be alive. Two raving maniacs in a Jensen nearly ran over me at your front gate.
Niamh But that must have been——
Grainne (*shutting her up*) —terrible for you.
Usheen They ought to be locked up. Then I fell into a bloody great hole out there.
Grainne That's going to be our swimming-pool.
Usheen (*coldly*) Oh, yes?
Grainne Heated.
Niamh You're lucky—next month you would have drowned.
Usheen (*eyeing her bleakly*) Have we met?
Grainne Excuse me—this is Niamh Kinnore. Niamh is my very dearest friend—we've known each other a week.
Usheen Charmed.
Niamh I watch you every Sunday, Mr Usheen. I don't know how you think up all the——
Usheen Could we move out of here, or are we rehearsing for a Japanese wedding?
Grainne Of course, James.
Niamh (*lamely*) —all those funny rude remarks you make.

They move back into the living-room. Usheen brings the brandy bottle with him

Usheen Have you just had visitors?
Grainne Why do you ask?
Usheen That Jensen was coming out of your drive,

Grainne Was it? Sometimes cars use our gateway to turn in. Did you get the number?

Usheen No——

Grainne What a pity.

Usheen —but just before I threw myself into your flower-bed I saw the ugly red face of the bastard who was driving. He said, "I'll kill her, I'll kill her" . . .

Niamh Why would Fintan want to . . .

Grainne Heavens, look at your coat. Take it off, James. (*She assists him*)

Usheen I suppose he mistook me for a woman. I never forget a face, and I won't forget that one.

Niamh (*a golden-tongued flatterer*) I would never mistake you for a woman, Mr Usheen.

Usheen You're a perceptive little thing, aren't you? Yes, I'll remember that git. And if I ever meet him . . . !

Grainne My goodness, what a beautiful coat.

Usheen Think so? I bought it to spite Eamonn Andrews. Now it's ruined.

Grainne No, it's only mud. It'll brush out. The important thing is, you got here.

Usheen Where's your husband?

Grainne He—went to Cork.

Usheen Oh?

Grainne Unexpectedly.

Usheen I'm sorry to have missed him.

Grainne So I'm afraid we're all alone.

Usheen You and I?

Grainne Yes.

Usheen What's *that*, then?

They both look at Niamh, who has been drinking in every word

Niamh, why don't you take James's coat somewhere and see what you can do with it?

Niamh Will I hang on here until it's dry?

Grainne No, dear.

Niamh Well, will I come straight back?

Grainne (*shaking her head slowly and deliberately*) Of course come straight back.

Niamh reluctantly takes the coat and goes to the door

(*To Usheen, smiling*) Well!

Niamh Pssst!

Grainne (*to Usheen*) Excuse me. (*Going to Niamh*) What?

Niamh Be careful.

Grainne Clean the coat.

Niamh I suppose, coming from England, he's on the Pill?

Grainne The coat, Niamh.

Niamh Make sure.

Niamh goes out unwillingly

Grainne comes down to Usheen. They face each other

Usheen Well!
Grainne (*smiling*) Well?

He starts towards her. She prepares herself for a blissful encounter, but he bypasses her. His destination is the brandy bottle

Do please help yourself.
Usheen Do you realize, this brandy has probably been in cask since the last time I saw you?
Grainne Twelve years.
Usheen Is it? (*Sniffing the brandy*) You're right, you know!
Grainne You've said hello to it twice—you might say hello to me. How do I look?
Usheen Superb.
Grainne (*pleased*) Liar.
Usheen The prettiest brunette on our road. You still are.
Grainne There's mud on your glasses.
Usheen Is there? (*He takes them off*) Oh, my God!
Grainne (*touching her hair*) I wouldn't have changed it, but Dermod likes me in red.
Usheen Oh, yes?
Grainne He says it'll remind us of the days when we had an overdraft. God has been so good to us since then.
Usheen I do congratulate Him.
Grainne Do you, James? Some men might be disappointed. Some men might wish that a girl hadn't done quite so well for herself without him.
Usheen I couldn't be more thrilled.
Grainne Thank you, James.
Usheen And that dress!
Grainne This old thing? It's my newest.
Usheen It'll be a knockout when it's finished.
Grainne I like your suit.
Usheen Good.
Grainne One of dozens?
Usheen I have six . . .
Grainne Dermod has ten.
Usheen Beige, that is.
Grainne Speaking of handmade shoes . . .
Usheen (*looking at a painting*) That is beautiful.
Grainne What? Oh yes, we like that.
Usheen I love it.
Grainne It's a Paul Henry (*or whatever*)
Usheen I know. I have the original.
Grainne Oh?
Usheen Somewhere.

Grainne Well, we've both come a long way.

Usheen Would you say?

Grainne You, especially.

Usheen Yes, I suppose I have.

Grainne But then, of course, I didn't have nearly so far to travel.

Usheen You're beautiful when you smile.

Grainne Am I, James?

Usheen Are those your own teeth?

Grainne Seriously, James, Dermod and I are two of your most devoted fans. We've watched every programme of yours right from the very beginning.

Usheen All of them?

Grainne I swear.

Usheen Good God.

Grainne Except one.

Usheen How super.

Grainne Yes.

Usheen Fantastic.

Grainne Mmmm.

Usheen How come you missed one?

Grainne We switched over to Eamonn Andrews. More brandy? (*She sails into the bar*) I got him, I got him, I got him!

Usheen Grainne!

Grainne Com-ing!

Usheen I am going home.

Grainne He's going home.

Usheen Good-bye.

Grainne Good—bye!

Usheen stomps out

Good-bye? My God, I must have been mad. James, come back.

Usheen returns

Usheen Where is my overcoat?

Grainne I was joking.

Usheen You were not.

Grainne I was.

Usheen There are two things one does not joke about—death and Eamonn Andrews.

Grainne So it was a joke in poor taste.

Usheen Sick.

Grainne The reason I missed your programme just that once was because the children had tonsilitis.

Usheen And that is your excuse?

Grainne We thought they were dying.

Usheen That's better,

Grainne Of course it is.

Usheen I'll buy that.

Grainne So sit, have your drink and talk to me.

Usheen Yes, when I met your husband in London he mentioned you had children.

Grainne Two. Emer and Ronan.

Usheen Where are the little bug—beggars?

Grainne They're convalescing at the moment with friends of ours who have a house in Greece.

Usheen I like Greece.

Grainne So do we.

Usheen For week-ends.

There is a moment of strain

Grainne Pax, James.

Usheen Pax. Your husband seems a nice fellow.

Grainne Yes, doesn't he!

Usheen I suppose you're mad about him.

Grainne I adore him. But let's not talk about what's-his-name—Dermod —and me. Especially not me. All I am is just a plain, dull, boring house-wife.

Usheen smiles to himself and nods his head. When she looks at him, the nod turns into a shake

Tell me what you've been up to. (*Playfully*) I've heard the most shocking stories.

Usheen About me?

Grainne And women. I'm afraid you're a wicked man.

Usheen Ha-ha.

Grainne And here I am alone in the house at your mercy.

Usheen Isn't your friend still here?

Grainne She won't come in—not unless she heard me screaming the place down.

Usheen Well, then!

Grainne (*eyeing him firmly*) I never scream.

For a moment Usheen is stunned by the implications of this

Usheen I see! What you mean is, there won't be any need for you to scream, because you can trust me. Thank you—and yes, yes, you can!

Grainne Can what?

Usheen Trust me.

Grainne Yes?

Usheen You are the one woman I will always respect.

Grainne Oh, shit. (*She bursts into tears. Grainne is a noisy weeper*)

Usheen Why, I'd sooner lose my Sunday-night TAM ratings than harm a hair of your head. (*He pats her head*) There, there, there! No need to snivel. To me, you'll always be the shy little girl who used to shudder with virginal passion whenever I touched her. You're as safe with me now as you were then. Of course, I'm only human. The best of men sometimes commit the most horrible deeds.

At this ray of hope, Grainne stops crying

They kill the things they love—perhaps through frailty, perhaps in a fit of drunkenness.

Grainne at once pours him a drink and puts it firmly in his hand

But if I were to utter one lustful word to you, drunk or sober, I hope I should drop dead. Thanks. (*He drinks*) I'm not a virtuous man. You may as well know that what they say about me is true. I have had women —in a way.

Grainne How interesting. (*Delicately*) Which way did you have them?

Usheen And yet, through the whole ugly, sordid mess, there was always one woman I truly loved.

Grainne (*overwhelmed*) Do you mean . . . ?

Usheen One person who meant everything to me.

Grainne Oh, James.

Usheen A love that stayed fine throughout the years.

Grainne Don't . . .

Usheen Her name was Venetia.

He misinterprets Grainne's stunned reaction

And you're right—bloody stupid name for a woman. The silly cow liked to pretend she'd been conceived in a gondola. You read about the divorce case I was mixed up in? She was the woman. Afterwards, we lived together. Openly. Convention thrown to the winds, lost to all sense of shame, God no longer existed.

Grainne Why didn't you marry her?

Usheen Are you mad? Marry a divorced woman—and be excommunicated? You're not paying attention, are you? Get the wax out, there's a good girl. Where was I?

Grainne Venetia.

Usheen Don't mention that woman's name to me.

Grainne But didn't you love her?

Usheen I curse the day I first laid hands on her. Three o'clock in the morning—"James, do you love me?" I reply tenderly (*snarling*) "I'm in bed with you amn't I?" Do you think that satisfies her? No, she wants more endearments, and then it's "You don't love me, you don't. And I broke up my marriage for you." Her marriage! Her husband was a fifty-three-year-old alcoholic who narrowly escaped prosecution on a charge of attempted misconduct with a pillar-box while under the impression that it was a Chinese streetwalker. And that's the kind of anatomical education you pick up at Eton! Oh, those four words— "You don't love me!"—the great digestive belch of a woman who's been feeding on your entrails. Then, after the recriminations, the threats. "I'll give myself to the first man I meet."

Grainne (*taking his now empty glass*) Did she?

Usheen She tried it once. Disappeared. Of course I knew where to find her. Seven a.m., and she was in Chiswick, walking up and down outside Eamonn Andrews' gate. Silly cow, didn't even know he'd moved. And after the threats, the worst part.

Grainne What was that? (*She begins to refill his glass*)

Usheen She . . . (*his voice breaks*)

Grainne She tried to kill herself.

Usheen Worse. She did what was unforgivable.

Grainne Tell me.

Usheen If you'll shut up for a minute, I will. She was rude to me.

Grainne Oh.

Usheen Insults, sarcasm, nasty little gibes. She said I had a big head and a small—oh, but some people have wicked tongues. Do you know what that woman did? She castrated me.

Grainne considers this, then regretfully begins to pour his brandy back into the bottle

Figuratively speaking.

Grainne pours the brandy back into the glass.

Grainne Did you leave her?

Usheen Regularly. I took up with those other women you just now mentioned. I didn't need her, and I'd prove it. The trouble was, when it came right down to the nitty-gritty—I couldn't.

Grainne You couldn't what?

Usheen I just—couldn't. Perhaps I'd had too much to drink at the time. Perhaps that was why.

Grainne sighs, looks at the brandy and once more pours it from the glass back into the bottle

No—no, it wasn't.

Grainne gives him both bottle and glass and lets him do his own pouring

At the moment of truth, the same thing always happened. I kept seeing her mole.

Grainne Her what?

Usheen She had a large mole right here—(*he prods his chest then prods Grainne's*)—there. I beg your pardon.

Grainne My pleasure.

Usheen I kept seeing her mole—her beauty spot, she called it. Ugly-looking thing. It ruined my life. Three weeks ago, I made up my mind, left her for good. It's over now.

Grainne Venetia and you?

Usheen Everything. Involvements, emotions, sex. I've finished with it all.

Niamh's voice is heard off

Niamh Oh, Jay.

Usheen opens the door and reveals Niamh kneeling at the keyhole

Excuse me. The television set in the kitchen isn't working.
Grainne (*stunned, still looking at Usheen*) Try the one in the loo.

Usheen closes the door

Usheen I'm sorry—this must be distressing for you.
Grainne You have no idea.
Usheen It's my own fault. I should have fallen in love with an Irish girl.
Grainne An Irish girl might have had a mole, too.
Usheen Yes, but I'd never have seen it.
Grainne If you believe that, you've been away for longer than you think.
Usheen (*shaking his head*) Some things never change. That's why I came
to see you—my first love. The girl who longed to be a nun.
Grainne Did I say that?
Usheen Have you forgotten? That was the reason you gave for not wanting
to see me any more.
Grainne (*remembering*) So it was.
Usheen If I'm going to embark upon a life of celibacy, I thought I should
begin here, with the only truly pure girl I ever knew.
Grainne Me?

*Tongue-tied with emotion, he cocks a finger at her like a pistol and fires an
imaginary shot by way of an affirmative*

Did you really love me, James?
Usheen I adored every black hair on your red head. I mean I . . .
Grainne (*swallowing this*) And I was fond of *you*, James. I still am, and
I'm not going to stand by and watch you let a tiny mole ruin your life.
Usheen It was a brute of a mole. And what can you do?
Grainne Supposing you were to slip on our imported Hong Kong marble
bathroom floor and break your back? You'd expect me to help, wouldn't
you? You'd expect me to—to do whatever it is you would do for a
broken back.
Usheen Yes, but . . .
Grainne This is the same thing. You're still moping over that awful woman,
and I think what you need is a—love transplant.

Usheen is about to speak

Don't argue—I am a woman, and that means I'm wonderfully wise, and
I know that perfect love, and perfect love alone, casteth out moles.
James, I have something to show you.
Usheen (*nervously*) Oh?
Grainne Right now.
Usheen (*his eyes on her bosom*) I don't think I want to . . .
Grainne You'll love it. It's the most beautiful mo——
Usheen I won't look.
Grainne —motel in the world. Dermod owns it—at least he owns half of
it. Let's go there.
Usheen To a motel? What for?
Grainne I'll tell you on the way. It's only up the mountains.

Usheen Up the . . . ?

Grainne The view is marvellous.

Usheen It's pitch dark out, it's pouring rain and there's a gale blowing.

Grainne Irish weather, James—what they call a soft night. (*This strikes her as humorous, she giggles*)

Usheen But what has you showing me a motel got to do with Venetia's mole?

Grainne No questions. You must put yourself completely in my hands. Don't move, I'll get my coat.

Usheen Couldn't we just sit here and . . .

Grainne goes out

Usheen remains seated, looking baffled

A motel? Why does she want us to . . . (*The truth dawns*) She wouldn't! (*Discarding the idea as preposterous*) Don't be a fool, James, lad—she's an Irish Catholic wife and mother. The only thing she's got left is her virginity. (*He rises and takes a step towards the door, calling*) Grainne, I . . . (*He stops. A look of physical discomfort comes over his face. He touches his trouser-legs*) Damn.

Grainne swings back into the room, now wearing a mink coat. She remembers to model it for us briefly, humming "A Pretty Girl is like a Melody". She passes the stricken Usheen on her way to the bar

Grainne I threw on just any old thing.

Usheen Grainne . . .

Grainne resumes humming and goes into the bar. Ducking expertly, she picks up two bottles of brandy and comes out at once, ducking again

Usheen Grainne, I can't go.

Grainne Yes, you can.

Usheen There's something you don't know.

Grainne About Venetia?

Usheen About me. (*Indicating his upper leg*) Touch me here.

Grainne Later, James.

Usheen I mean I'm soaked to the skin.

Grainne For heaven's sake, a little dampness . . . !

Usheen Oh, if ever I get my hands on that red-faced bastard in the Jensen . . . !

Grainne Take off your trousers.

Usheen I beg your pardon?

Grainne You can borrow a pair of Dermod's.

Usheen But . . .

Grainne Or do you *want* to catch cold? (*She goes to the door and calls off*) Niamh, is Mr Usheen's overcoat dry yet? (*To Usheen*) Will you do as you're told? Take them *off*.

Grainne goes out

Usheen broods for a moment, then reluctantly removes his trousers. He begins to empty the pockets

Niamh comes in with his overcoat. The sight of Usheen, trouserless, stops her dead in her tracks

Niamh *Already?*

Usheen My trousers got wet.

Niamh (*with a forced smile*) Ah, sure why wouldn't they!

There is an embarrassed pause. Usheen toys with his drink. Niamh tries unsuccessfully to keep her eyes away from his shorts. Their eyes meet

Terrible weather.

Usheen (*shortly*) Yes.

Niamh You'd need those on you this evening.

Usheen I'm sure.

Niamh I like blue.

Usheen contrives to hide his shorts from view

Fintan won't wear them. He says they're unmanly. So I'm always at him.

Usheen looks at her

To wear drawers, I mean. If you were him now and I was another woman, there'd be a court case. Can I ask you something, Mr Usheen?

Usheen No.

Niamh I might never get the chance again, so just as a favour would you say something insulting?

Usheen (*losing his temper*) Bugger off.

Niamh Ah, thanks.

Grainne comes back with a pair of trousers

Grainne These are just back from the cleaners. Put them on.

Usheen Grainne, perhaps we should give the motel a miss for this evening. It's getting late, and . . .

Grainne Late? The night is still a pup. Now put them on. We won't look —(*to Niamh*)—will we?

Grainne and Niamh retire to a position behind Usheen and watch fascinated as he puts on the trousers. Through the following they keep their eyes on him

Niamh Grainne . . .

Grainne What?

Niamh Be good, will you?

Grainne I'll be magnificent.

Niamh moans feebly

Now listen. Leave his wet trousers on the radiator in the kitchen.
Niamh Right.
Grainne And when we're gone, ring up the motel. Tell the caretaker
you're me. Say that two married friends of yours are on their way there.
They need a room, and he's to let them in. Got that?
Usheen Blast.
Grainne What's wrong?
Usheen The zip's stuck.
Grainne That's what dry cleaning does. Pull it.
Usheen I am—it's stuck.
Grainne Soap will fix it. Wait . . .

Grainne goes out

*Usheen pulls on the zip. Niamh kneels down in front of him and peers closely
at the zip*

Usheen What are you doing?
Niamh Let me have a go—I'm great with lids. Hold still.

*As Niamh wrestles with the zip, still kneeling in front of Usheen, Fintan
appears outside the french windows. He clutches his face in horror at what
he thinks he sees, then bangs on the glass with his fists*

Do you hear the wind?
Usheen That doesn't sound like . . .
Niamh There, I've got it.

*Fintan, grabbing his hair in fury, goes tearing off around the side of the
house*

(*Yelling*) Grainne, come back, I've got it!
Usheen Thank you, and bless your little frankfurter fingers. My overcoat?
Niamh It's here. (*She helps him on with his coat*)

Grainne returns

Grainne Is he unfastened?
Niamh Yes.
Grainne (*picking up the brandy*) Then let's go. Niamh, you know what to
do.
Niamh Yes. No. I don't know the number of the—(*looking at Usheen*)—
M-O-T-T-E-L.
Usheen Mottel?
Grainne It's in Dermod's address book. In the study, across the hall.
(*Taking Usheen's arm*) 'Bye, now.
Usheen Are you sure this excursion is necessary?
Grainne I'll be the judge of that, James. You just keep on repeating as
we drive—"There are no moles on Grainne".

Usheen Pardon?
Grainne You heard.

Grainne crosses herself and pushes Usheen out ahead of her

Niamh 'Bye, 'bye, now. Have a nice . . . (*Getting on safer ground*) 'Bye!

The front door slams
Niamh wavers for a moment

Address book!

*Niamh goes out at the very moment when Fintan reappears at the window,
now brandishing a hatchet. He smashes the lock on the french windows
with one blow, then bursts into the room waving the hatchet. His hair is
flattened by the rain*

Fintan (*triumphantly*) Gotcha! (*He realizes that the room is empty. Then
his eyes focus on the bar. He emits a growling noise and rushes in. We
expect him to bang his head, but he ducks just in time and stands inside the
bar, crouching*)

Dermod comes in by the french windows, noting the shattered lock

Dermod (*sharply*) Fintan!

Fintan jerks upright and bangs his head on the ceiling

Fintan Jasus.
Dermod Come out here. Did you break that lock?
Fintan (*dazed*) What?
Dermod And where did you get that hatchet?
Fintan In your shed.
Dermod That shed was locked.
Fintan I broke the lock.
Dermod What for?
Fintan To get the hatchet to break *that* lock. (*He indicates the french
window*) Why else do you think I broke the branch off the tree?
Dermod What tree?
Fintan (*pointing out*) *That* tree!
Dermod My cherry tree?
Fintan God, didn't I need the branch to break the lock of the shed to get
the hatchet to break *that* lock? (*To the audience*) He's so thick. And she's
upstairs now.
Dermod Who is?
Fintan Niamh. I saw her through the window. She was . . .
Dermod She was what?
Fintan Kneeling down.
Dermod Praying?
Fintan If she was, it wasn't for a mild winter.
Dermod What was she doing?

Fintan I won't tell you. I wouldn't tell anyone. It's a mortal sin even to *know* what she was doing. There was this man . . .

Dermod What man?

Fintan And I know his face from somewhere. He . . .

Dermod Niamh and a man? You're raving.

Fintan I tell you they're upstairs. My God, if they'd do what I saw them doing in a living-room, what are they not perpetrating in the presence of a bed? I'll kill her.

Dermod Fintan, your wife is not in this house.

Fintan She's bouncing on your springs.

Dermod She's gone.

Fintan Get stitched.

Dermod While you were pulling up my good tree, Grainne's car went out the gate. She and Niamh have gone to your house for the night, as they were supposed to.

Fintan (*hollowly*) He's taken her off to some whorehouse!

Dermod There was no man here with Niamh.

Fintan I saw him.

Dermod You saw Grainne.

Fintan Your wife is ugly, but I wouldn't mistake her for a man.

Dermod (*blinking*) My wife is ugly?

Fintan I know, but don't dwell on it.

Dermod (*losing his temper*) That does it!

Fintan Does what?

Dermod I let you drag me back, all the way from Terenure, because it's either end up in bits on the motorway or let you see for yourself that Niamh is here and up to no harm. So I wait in the car, and what's my thanks? You break my cherry tree, you smash the lock on my shed, you butcher my french windows, and now you insult my wife. And all because your brain is unhinged.

Fintan Say that again!

Dermod You're having hallucinations.

Fintan You pup, you.

Dermod There was no man in this room.

Fintan (*almost dancing with fury*) I saw him, I saw him!

Dermod You saw your reflection in the glass.

Fintan I saw my . . . (*He breaks off. It occurs to him that Dermod may be right*)

Dermod (*having won his point*) And now I'm going to have a drink. (*He goes into the bar*)

Fintan looks from the french windows to the spot where he saw Niamh and Usheen

Do you want one?

Fintan (*convinced*) He was a handsome bugger, right enough. Funny, the way your mind plays tricks. I could have sworn that I saw her kneeling down . . . (*He starts towards the bar, then sees Usheen's trousers on the back of a chair. He picks them up, discovers that they are wet and drops* *them with a gasp of revulsion. He heads into the bar)* So I'm imagining things, am I?

Dermod *(wearily)* Oh, God.

Fintan Am I imagining a pair of trousers? A pair of *wet* trousers?

Dermod You're demented.

Fintan Is that so? Come out and look.

Niamh returns with the address book. She goes towards the telephone, then notices the trousers. She picks them up and goes out with them

Dermod Look at what?

Fintan The trousers.

Dermod Whose?

Fintan His. They're in there, and they're sopping wet.

Dermod Trousers?

Fintan He couldn't even wait to drop them till he got upstairs.

Dermod Why are they wet?

Fintan Don't ask me. Will you come and look?

Dermod Damn sure I'll come and look.

Niamh disappears with the trousers a split second before they emerge from the bar

Fintan Now we'll see who's demented. *(He points to the chair)* There!

Dermod Where?

Fintan *There*—are you . . . *(He stares at the empty chair. He goes on his knees and looks under it, then runs his hands over the chair, as if the trousers were still on it, but had turned invisible)* They were here ten seconds ago.

Dermod Fintan, see a doctor.

Fintan I saw them, I touched them. They were wet. Feel my hand.

Dermod *(doing so)* Your hand is dry.

Fintan Of course it's bloody dry—I wiped it!

Dermod Fintan, go home, go to bed.

Fintan *(jumping up and down, almost weeping with rage)* I saw the bugger's trousers, I saw them, I saw them.

Dermod Fintan, stop that.

Fintan I did, I did, I did. *(He gives three more mighty jumps as he speaks)*

Dermod You'll upset all the thermostats.

Fintan *(with sudden cunning)* I know what it is. It's a plot to drive me mad.

Dermod Now, look . . .

Fintan You're behind it—you and that ugly wife of yours. You want the Cork motel for yourself.

Dermod *(coldly)* I think we should forget about the Cork motel for the time being. Perhaps our partnership wasn't such a good idea after all.

Fintan There's no perhaps about it.

Dermod Seeing trousers that aren't there, I can understand. But *wet* trousers—that's sick.

Fintan *You'll* be sick in a minute. (*He looks about wildly for the hatchet*)

Dermod sees the hatchet at the same time, and they both make a rush for it. Dermod gets there first

Dermod (*loftily*) My hatchet, I believe.

Fintan What else could I expect from a get who got where he is by informing on people to the Income Tax.

Dermod Earlier, you said you wished you'd thought of it first.

Fintan (*massively*) *That* was common politeness.

Dermod (*dignified*) Fintan, I wish you good night.

Fintan There's no harm in wishing.

Dermod I mean good-bye.

Fintan The only place I'm going is up your stairs. That's where my wife is, and there's a man with her with his trousers off.

Dermod If I go up and look, will that convince you?

Fintan I wouldn't believe you if you told me that Paisley was a Protestant. Give me that hatchet.

Dermod I'll keep the hatchet, Fintan.

Dermod goes out

Fintan is on the point of following him, but decides that he needs a weapon. He goes into the bar and picks up a bottle which he strikes viciously into the palm of his hand. He discards it in favour of a heavy decanter which he holds like a cudgel

Niamh comes in carrying the address book and humming loudly to herself. She goes to the telephone and dials

Fintan, hearing the humming, looks puzzled and rotates a finger in his ear to get rid of it

Niamh (*shrilling*) "Let me call you sweetheart, I'm in love with you; let me hear you whisper that you love me too . . ." (*Into the phone*) Hello, is that the Patrick Pearse Motel? . . . Are you the caretaker? This is Mrs Dermod Gibbon speaking.

Fintan sticks his head around the door of the bar to look at Niamh

I'm well, and how are you? . . . Aren't you great. The thing is, there are two friends of mine who need a room for tonight, and I'm sending them up to the motel . . . Yes, so it's all right to let them in . . . A lady and a gentleman, yes . . . No, not a twin, I think they'd like a double. The main thing is, you'll be ready for them?

Fintan nods slowly, and with emphasis

Thanks very much . . . Not at all. Good-bye.

Niamh hangs up, looks heavenwards for forgiveness, and goes out, humming again

Fintan emerges from the bar

Fintan Oh, the rip. Lust under the Plough and the Stars—there's not a jury in the country will convict me. What are you talking about? You'll be made a Papal Count. But the rip!

Dermod returns

Dermod There's no-one upstairs, not a soul. Go and see for yourself.
Fintan Your word is good enough for me.
Dermod I'm not accustomed to being called a . . . Pardon?
Fintan (*elaborately casual*) It seems I was mistaken. I'll go home, so—home to bed.
Dermod Fintan, are you all right?
Fintan Me? How can I be all right? I imagine things. I'm demented, I'm sick.
Dermod If I said anything in haste . . .
Fintan (*airily*) Don't give it a thought. I dare say we'll meet again. And if we don't, sure our solicitors will.

Fintan gives Dermod a nod from a great height and goes out

Dermod Solicitors? I always knew he had a slate loose. Failure has gone to his head. (*He removes his coat, aware that he is in for a solitary evening. He goes up to the hi-fi unit and sets about selecting a record*)

As Dermod puts the record on the turntable, Niamh comes in, dressed for home. She is about to switch off the lights when she sees Dermod with his back to her. She emits a hoarse cry of shock, then goes haring out again

Dermod turns, just in time not to see her. He goes towards the door

Dermod Who's that? Who is it, who's there? (*Looking into the hall*) You? What are *you* doing here?

Miss Manning comes in, smiling the smile of modest achievement. She wears spectacles, her hair is drawn back severely into a bun. Her coat and galoshes are sensible. She has the habit of saying "Ai" and "mai" instead of "I" and "my"

Miss Manning How nice to see you again, Mr Gibbon. Wasn't I expected?
Dermod Not tonight, Miss Manning. They told me London Airport was closed.
Miss Manning It is. I took a train to Manchester and an aeroplane from there. A good employee can always find a way.
Dermod I congratulate you.
Miss Manning Might I compliment you, Mr Gibbon, upon the vigour of your friends?
Dermod Pardon me?

Miss Manning I was almost bowled over in your driveway by a gentleman who was running like billy-o.

Dermod That would have been my partner, Mr Kinnore. Running, did you say?

Miss Manning And again in your hall by a lady in a tizz.

Dermod A lady?

Miss Manning I'm sure you know best, Mr Gibbon.

Dermod Do sit down, Miss Manning. Did you have a good journey?

Miss Manning Beastly. On the train, I had to move my seat three times. Men with roving eyes, you know. No roving eyes here, Mr Gibbon.

Dermod (*with a forced smile*) Well, just a few.

She gives a genteel little laugh, which turns into a no less genteel cough

Miss Manning Hem! Might I have a glass of water?

Dermod Of course. Perhaps something a little stronger?

Miss Manning Well . . . ?

Dermod Whiskey?

Miss Manning Brandy?

Dermod (*taken slightly aback*) Certainly. (*He goes to the bar*) Odd—the brandy seems to have disappeared, Miss Manning. There's only Scotch.

Miss Manning I'm not fussy. (*She looks at him appraisingly as he pours her drink*) I went directly to my hotel, but they seem to have cancelled my reservation. So I'm open to suggestions.

Dermod Well, I . . .

Miss Manning Such a charming home. Perhaps I might impose on Mrs Gibbon and you for the night?

Dermod My wife is staying with a friend.

Miss Manning Oh? (*Receiving her drink*) 'nk yow!

Dermod So it would hardly be proper if . . .

Miss Manning Quite. We must be proper, mustn't we? (*She knocks back half her drink in one go*) I seem to be a little problem.

Dermod Not at all.

Miss Manning All I ask for is a bed. Then, first thing in the morning, I can begin my duties.

Dermod (*inspired*) But of course!

Miss Manning Yes?

Dermod The motel! You'll be staying there tomorrow anyway when the staff arrive. Why not tonight?

Miss Manning How super.

Dermod The only thing is, it's a bit isolated.

Miss Manning I don't mind loneliness. I was married for five years.

Dermod Oh, yes?

Miss Manning Horrid man. I shall adore being at the motel. Tomorrow morning I shall say to myself, "Here you are in Ireland, the land of creamery butter, little boggy roads, and religious mania." I've done my homework, you see!

Dermod Ha-ha.

Miss Manning Might we go now?

Dermod To the motel? Yes. Have you luggage?
Miss Manning I left it on the doorstep.
Dermod It'll get soaked there. I'll put it in the car. You finish your drink.
Miss Manning Too kind.

Dermod takes his coat and goes out

Miss Manning knocks back her drink, then helps herself to a refill, a hefty one. Carrying her glass, she drifts over to the hi-fi unit. She switches on the record player. The music is modern, sensuous

Miss Manning Irish music—how super! (*She continues her tour of the room, drinking as she goes. Gradually, and apparently without realizing it, she begins to move in rhythm with the music. She opens a button of her coat, then shrugs one shoulder free, then the other. The coat falls to the floor and she steps out of it. She undoes the bow holding her hair in place, then shakes her head and lets her hair fall about her shoulders. Her mind seems to be a thousand miles away, but her body is getting into the spirit of the music. She takes off her glasses. She begins to unbutton her blouse*)

Dermod comes in and stands stock still

Swaying sinuously, Miss Manning now unzips her skirt. She sees Dermod and zips it up again, taking her time and not the least embarrassed. She switches off the record player

Miss Manning I find music ever so restful, don't you?
Dermod (*croaking*) Yes.
Miss Manning Is something not right?
Dermod No. You don't seem quite the same as you did in London.
Miss Manning Gentlemen often say that about me—that I'm different. I don't know why. I hope I won't be a disappointment to you, Mr Gibbon.
Dermod I'm sure you won't.
Miss Manning And I know *I'm* going to enjoy working for *you*. I haven't had an interesting position since before my marriage, and it's so important to a girl as to whom she is under.
Dermod Oh, yes?
Miss Manning Will Mrs Gibbon be away *all* night?
Dermod Yes.
Miss Manning Oh, poor thing.
Dermod I'm supposed to be in Cork.
Miss Manning And amn't I glad you aren't!
Dermod Shall we go now?
Miss Manning Super. I can't wait. (*She gives him her coat to hold, and puts it on*) 'nk yow! Now I'm all yours.

She turns so that she is very close to him. He is on the point of losing control, when she moves away from him abruptly and goes towards the door

Are you partial to animals, Mr Gibbon?

Dermod Animals, Miss Manning?

Miss Manning Call me Venetia. I have the prettiest mole you have ever seen.

Miss Manning goes out as Dermod takes a step to follow her, and—

the CURTAIN *falls*

ACT II

SCENE 1

The Motel. Fifteen minutes later

We see two bedrooms and a section of corridor. Seen from above, the corridor would resemble a letter "H" lying on its side. It runs from R to L up stage, and parallel to this down stage. A connecting length of corridor C cuts the stage in two and separates the two bedrooms. These are the Emmet room and the Parnell room. Each room is a mirror image of the other, except that one contains a large oil painting of Charles Stewart Parnell, and the other one of Robert Emmet. Each room contains a double bed, built-in wardrobe, easy chair and chest-of-drawers. Bathrooms are situated off down stage on either side

As the Curtain rises,.Hoolihan, the night watchman, appears in the corridor, followed by Grainne and Usheen. He is in his late seventies

Hoolihan Now this, sir and missus, is what they call the Nineteenth Century wing. (*He indicates the doors at the rear*) There's a lovely room, the Isaac Butt room. And next to it, the Manchester Martyrs' room, with three single beds. You don't want that.

Usheen He's made a mistake. Tell him we're not staying.

Hoolihan Yes, sir, sure they're all lovely rooms. And this one, excuse me, sir and missus—is the Chief's room . . .

Usheen The old eejit thinks we're staying the night.

Hoolihan goes into the Parnell room, salutes the painting, and stands before it at attention

Hoolihan Charles Stewart Parnell!

Usheen This isn't a motel. It's Madame Tussauds.

Grainne Be respectful, James. He was out in nineteen-sixteen.

Usheen By the look of him, he hasn't come in yet. Let's get away from here now.

Grainne James, it's time you and I had our little talk.

Usheen Right, we can have it back at your place—I've got to pick up my trousers anyway.

Grainne But . . .

Hoolihan, having again saluted, comes out

Hoolihan Now I'll show you another lovely room. Named after bold Robert Emmet, sir, the darlin' of Erin. (*He goes into the Emmet room, salutes the portrait and stands before it in homage*)

Usheen He's doing it again. My God, it's a political Stations of the Cross. How many rooms in this madhouse?
Grainne Eighty-four.
Usheen We'll be here all bloody night.
Grainne (*with a catlike smile*) Mmmm . . .
Usheen What does that mean? ·

Hoolihan comes out

We're obliged to you for your trouble. This lady and I must be off now.
Hoolihan It is, it is. The next room is the Wolfe Tone room and the O'Donovan Rossa room . . .
Usheen He's senile.
Grainne Well, he's old.
Usheen That's no excuse.
Hoolihan (*tottering forward*) Hup, two, three three, four! Hup, two, three, four!
Grainne We'll give him the slip in a minute—you just be ready.

Hoolihan turns, waiting for them

We're com-ing!
Hoolihan Then there's the Thomas Davis room and the Michael Davitt room.

Hoolihan goes out of sight down left, followed by Usheen and Grainne

(*Off*) All lovely snug rooms. Hup, two, three, four!

There is a pause

Grainne (*off*) Now, James.

Grainne comes back into view, pausing for a moment, apparently leading an unseen Usheen by the hand

Don't hang back, he'll see us. (*She pulls, not Usheen, but Hoolihan into view and drags him after her at an agonized trot*) Any room will do us. In here—quickly. (*She drags him after her into the Parnell room and shuts the door*)

Hoolihan looks dazedly at his hand

There, we did it. (*She turns and sees him*) Oh, my God.
Hoolihan You squezz me hand.
Grainne I what?
Hoolihan The modern girls is very rough.

Usheen comes into view looking for Grainne

Usheen (*calling*) Grainne?

He goes off, right

Hoolihan You'd no call to go pulling and hauling at an old man and giving him a squezz hand. I'm seventy-eight, I have to be careful.

Grainne Yes, I'm sorry.

Hoolihan I have to go to the lav now over you.

Hoolihan shuffles into the bathroom. Grainne goes out and comes down stage

Grainne James, here I am. I made the silliest . . . (*She sees that he is gone*) James, where are you? James?

Grainne hesitates, then goes off left. Niamh appears at the rear, wandering along the corridor and carrying Usheen's trousers. She is looking for a sign of life and comes down stage

Niamh (*in a timid whisper*) Grainne? Mr Usheen? (*Very loudly*) Wooo-ooo!

Niamh goes out of sight up stage.
Grainne and Usheen enter down stage from opposite sides

Graine
Usheen } *There* you are!

Grainne Really, James, must you wander around? (*Going to him*) And if you want me, you know my name. There's no need to go "woo-ooo".

Usheen I didn't go "woo-hoo".

Grainne Come in here. (*She pushes him ahead of her into the Robert Emmet room*)

Usheen You're the one who went "woo-ooo".

Grainne Who did?

Usheen You did.

Grainne I did?

Usheen Just now, like a yak in labour.

Grainne (*bridling*) Wives of Members of the South Dublin Country Club are not in the habit of sounding like yaks in labour.

Usheen Then they must regard *you* as something of a novelty.

Grainne (*losing her temper*) James, I did not go . . .

Niamh appears up stage

Niamh Wooo-ooo!

Niamh goes off

Grainne Exactly. So . . . (*She breaks off*)

They look in the direction whence the cry came, then at each other

Usheen Then what the hell was it?

Grainne I don't know.

Usheen (*looking into the bathroom*) Perhaps it was the wind whistling through the bidets.

Grainne There aren't any bidets—Irish plumbers won't handle them.

Usheen In that case . . .

Grainne Well?

Usheen Do you think it could have been a yak?

Grainne James, there are no yaks in the Dublin Mountains.

Usheen There's *something* out there.

Grainne (*heatedly*) It isn't a yak.

Usheen Listen to me. I am a city boy. Where the footpaths stop, so do I, and I now wish to return to civilization.

Grainne James, we're fifteen miles from Foxrock. You can't *get* more civilized than that.

Usheen Did you hear that "woo-ooo"?

Grainne The wind.

Usheen It was not the wind. What a way for James Usheen to finish up— in a concrete tomb high up in these God-forsaken mountains, torn limb from limb by some kind of Abominable Bogman!

Grainne (*becoming frightened*) Now stop that.

Usheen It's out there now.

They hear the sound of Hoolihan as he emerges from the bathroom and passes through the Parnell room, clearing his throat loudly. Then he marches off up stage

Hoolihan Hup, two, three, four—hup, two, three, four!

Graine and Usheen breathe more easily

Grainne James, what's got into you?

Usheen I see it all with dreadful clarity. He hates me, he wants to kill me.

Grainne Who does?

Usheen So he sends two of his henchmen to run me down with a Jensen. Then I fall into a carefully dug pit. I survive that, and then, for no apparent reason, you take me up the mountains in a storm to a deserted bunker guarded by a madman. You work for Eamonn Andrews, don't you?

Grainne No!

Usheen Then why was I brought here?

Grainne (*decisively*) I'll show you. (*She removes her coat and lies on the bed invitingly*)

Usheen (*through this, to himself*) They all hate me.

Grainne Look at me, James. *Now* do you know why you were brought here?

He looks at her. Realization finally dawns

Usheen You're having me on.

Grainne Exactly.

Usheen You wouldn't.

Grainne I meant what I said, James. You've seen your last mole.

Usheen You'd do that for me?

Grainne (*simply*) What are friends for?

Niamh (*baying in the distance*) Wooo-ooo!

Grainne (*catching her breath*) There it is again.

Usheen Ignore it. (*Looking at her*) This is the nicest thing anyone ever offered to do for me.

Grainne It's purely medicinal.

Usheen Even so—I couldn't.

Grainne Why not?

Usheen You—who wanted to be a nun?

Grainne I wouldn't dream of enjoying it.

Usheen I know that, love.

Grainne I'm not immoral.

Usheen Sure.

Grainne Don't you find me attractive?

Usheen I'm mad about you. I always have been, but how could I do such a thing in your husband's trousers?

Grainne Silly—you won't be wearing them.

Usheen Besides, I've decided to return to my religion.

Grainne How soon?

Usheen Tomorrow.

Grainne Well, that gives us all night.

Usheen That's true. You really mean this?

Grainne Don't look so amazed. You'd do as much for me if I kept seeing moles on Dermod. Try thinking of it as laying a ghost.

Usheen When did you decide?

Grainne Quite on the spur of the moment. In the car.

Usheen It's ridiculous. I haven't even a toothbrush.

Grainne I have two in my handbag.

Usheen (*wiping his eyes*) What can I say, but that I accept gratefully, knowing that a refusal often gives offence.

Grainne (*kindly*) You need a drink. Where's the brandy?

Usheen You had it last.

Grainne I left it in the car. You wait here—I'll go out the back way, it's shorter.

Usheen Run.

Grainne hurries out

Usheen picks up her handbag, opens it and takes out the two toothbrushes. His eyes moisten with affection. Then he sees something else in the handbag. He pulls into view what looks like several yards of rolled-up, see-through black nylon nightdress. He holds it up, picturing Grainne in it

Niamh, footsore by now, comes into view, down stage still carrying

Usheen's trousers. She cups her hands over her mouth for another mighty yell

Usheen beats her to it. The sight of the nightdress causes him to emit a cry of sheer anticipation

Usheen Wooo-*ooo!*

Niamh looks puzzled. Usheen gleefully rolls up the nightdress and puts it back in the handbag. He takes off his overcoat and hangs it on a hook on the back of the half-open door. Niamh decides to investigate the source of the yell. She comes to the threshold of the Emmet room and looks in. She and Usheen are hidden from each other by the door. Seeing an apparently empty room, she goes out again, closing the door behind her. Usheen sees the door and his overcoat swinging from him. Niamh turns her attention to the Parnell room. She goes in, just as Ushen looks around the door of the Emmet room and sees nothing. Niamh's feet are killing her and she is dispirited. She sits on the bed and takes her shoes off. Simultaneously, in the other room, Usheen sits on the bed and removes his shoes. They emit independent sighs of relief and begin to massage their toes

Fintan appears up stage and stations himself between the two rooms. He is in a murderous mood

Fintan (*hissing off, impatiently*) Come on, come on, come on! Will you hurry up. I'm not paying you to sleep on your feet.

Hoolihan comes into view carrying a lethal-looking shillelagh

Is that the biggest shillelagh we have in the gift shop?
Hoolihan It's crooked.
Fintan It's meant to be crooked. What room did you say she pulled you into?
Hoolihan Funny-lookin' walkin'-stick.
Fintan For God's sake, man, can't you understand plain Irish? I'm talking about the woman.

Hoolihan looks at him blankly

Who pulled you into a bedroom?
Hoolihan She squezz me hand.
Fintan The whoor.
Hoolihan Hard.
Fintan Describe her to me.

Hoolihan merely holds up his hand

Would you call her a raving beauty?
Hoolihan I had to go to the lav over her.
Fintan I know that feeling—it's her all right. Which room did she go into? (*Grabbing him*) Which room?

Hoolihan (*saluting*) Charles Stewart Parnell.
Fintan Parnell. Of course—where else for adultery? Oh, the slut.

Usheen starts removing his jacket. Fintan, gripping the shillelagh, advances on tiptoe towards the Emmet room.

Hoolihan Bold Robert Emmet.
Fintan Shut up. (*Then he sees the nameplate on the door*) Oh.

Niamh puts her shoes on again and goes towards the bathroom. Fintan changes course for the Parnell room. Niamh enters the bathroom, closing the door. Fintan pounces in

Gotcha! (*He stops in frustration*)

Hoolihan comes in behind him. Usheen goes into the bathroom

Gone.
Hoolihan (*looking at the portrait of Parnell*) Gone—all of them gone.
Fintan Wait! (*He sees Usheen's trousers on the bed where Niamh has left them*) The same trousers I saw seven miles away—and they're still sopping wet! I don't know what it is, but there's a perverted act going on here somewhere.

Grainne reappears with the brandy. She goes into the Emmet room and opens one of the bottles, humming to herself

I'll search every room in the place from Brian Boru to Bernadette Devlin, and when I find them . . . !

Still holding the trousers, he hustles Hoolihan out ahead of him and off downstage. In his anger he has left the shillelagh on the bed.
Niamh, attracted by Fintan's final shout, comes out of the bathroom, dabbing at her face with a towel

Niamh Mr Usheen? (*She is about to return to the bathroom when she notices that Usheen's trousers have gone. She looks for them with mounting panic, but can find only the shillelagh*)

In the Emmet room, Grainne taps on the bathroom door

Grainne James, dear, are you in there?
Usheen (*off*) No.
Grainne Well, really, haven't you ever heard of ladies first? Never mind, I'll use one of the other bathrooms. (*She takes her handbag and goes out. She enters the Parnell room*)

Niamh is on her hands and knees looking for the lost trousers

Grainne goes into the bathroom without seeing Niamh. Niamh gives up the search and returns to the bathroom. She screams off, Grainne comes in, dragging Niamh after her with one hand and holding her nightdress in the other

Grainne Of all the mean things. How dare you come here and spy on us. Don't you know I'd have given you all the details tomorrow?

Niamh There's not going to be any details. Dermod's come home.

Grainne He's what?

Niamh I saw him.

Grainne The rotten thing.

Niamh And if he's at home, you may depend on it so is Fintan. There goes my night off.

Grainne Men! You can't trust them out of your sight.

Niamh So since you're supposed to be staying at my place, I came to collect you and give Mr Usheen back his trousers. Where is he?

Grainne (*pointing*) In there.

Niamh This will be a terrible let-down for him.

Grainne (*wincing*) Don't.

Niamh (*indicating the nightdress*) What's that?

Grainne My nightie.

Niamh (*fascinated by it*) A hell of a let-down.

Grainne I've been saving it for a rainy night.

Niamh (*examining it*) I suppose it's the same as sun-glasses, you can see everything through it, but it takes away the glare.

Grainne I'm furious with Dermod—my first evening out in ages, and he has to go and spoil it. Well, I won't let him. I've been to too much trouble, and waste is sinful.

Niamh You can't stay the whole night here—not now.

Grainne I'm aware of that. James will just have to put up with the abridged version.

Niamh Grainne, come home now.

Grainne *You* go home.

Niamh Without you?

Grainne Tell Fintan I'm following in my car. When I get there I'll say I had a puncture. Yes?

Niamh (*fearing the worst*) Oh, Jay.

Grainne And to prove I'm grateful, you can have that (*the nightdress*) tomorrow as a present. You can wear it for Fintan.

Niamh I'd never see the sun come up.

Grainne But please go *now*. Where are James's trousers?

Niamh They were here five minutes ago.

Grainne Well?

Niamh (*holding the shillelagh*) Now all I can find is this.

Grainne The night watchman must have taken them—what a funny old man. I'll find them. You go on home.

Grainne leads Niamh, still holding the shillelagh, into the corridor

Niamh How soon will you be after me?

Grainne As soon as I decently can. Now go. (*She goes into Emmet's room*)

Niamh The trousers might be under the bed.

Grainne closes the door. Niamh, left on her own, has no choice but to head for home. She comes down stage

(*Decisively*) Adultery can't be a sin—you go through so much suffering to commit it.

Niamh goes off

Grainne pours herself a brandy then goes to the bathroom door

Grainne James, are you still in there?

Usheen (*off*) The bloody zip is stuck again.

Grainne Well, do hurry. There's been some bad news. We're not playing a full eighteen holes any more. It's been changed to pitch-and-putt. Trousers . . . (*She takes her glass of brandy into the Parnell room, puts down the glass and looks under the bed*)

Niamh appears in the corridor, now in a state of yammering terror

Niamh Fintan's here, Fintan's here. (*She rushes into the Emmet room, assuming that Grainne is still there*) Grainne, we're nackered, it's F . . . (*She realizes that Grainne is no longer there. She tries the bathroom door. It is locked*)

Fintan and Hoolihan appear in the corridor

Niamh hammers on the bathroom door

Fintan's here—let me in.

Fintan The shillelagh was in your charge, do I have to see to everything myself?

Niamh (*hearing this*) He'll slaughter me.

Fintan (*close at hand*) It was this room. I know exactly where I left it.

Niamh assumes that he is about to enter the Emmet room. She utters a moan of "Oh, Jay," and begins to run around in circles like a decapitated hen, finally collapsing into the built-in wardrobe. At the same time, Fintan and Hoolihan go into the Parnell room, where Fintan looks wildly about him for his shillelagh, and Hoolihan comes to attention in front of the portrait of Parnell

In the Emmet room, Usheen comes out of the bathroom, his flies half undone

Usheen (*ranting*) What kind of a Communist country is this? Can't a man undo his fly in peace? (*Looking about him*) Grainne . . . ?

Fintan Gone—the shillelagh's gone. I'm going mad. I left it here, you saw me. (*He turns and sees Hoolihan*) Stop saluting that adulterer! Wait—I know where they are—(*pointing to the bathroom*)—in there! Easy now, Fintan, he's got a shillelagh.

Observed by Grainne from under the bed, Fintan charges into the bathroom

Grainne reaches for her nightdress which is lying on the floor. She draws it towards her. Hoolihan sees it moving. He tries to jump on it, and misses. He tries again and succeeds. He picks it up. At first he does not know what it is. Then dawn breaks. Usheen is meanwhile attacking the stuck zip with such fury that he is whirling about the room. He begins to cry with childish rage. Hoolihan holds the nightdress in front of himself and stands before the mirror

Hoolihan (*cackling*) Hih, hih, hih, hih!

Usheen Bugger it, bugger it, bugger it!

Fintan comes out of the bathroom, holding Grainne's fur coat

Fintan (*quietly; nothing else can happen*) Now I know. Now at last I know why she's doing it—for a mangy piece of rabbit skin.

The bed rocks violently. Fintan sits on it heavily

And for this she's willing to throw away a woman's most precious possession—her husband's social status. Well, I'll say this much in her favour—at least she's not doing it for love.

Hoolihan (*enjoying himself*) Hih, hih, hih, hih!

Fintan (*snarling*) What are you sniggering at? (*He sees the nightdress*) Show me that. (*He snatches it from Hoolihan*)

In the Emmet room, Usheen calms down

Usheen Steady, James love! You don't want to use up all your strength on a zip. Treat it as you would a studio audience. That's it—soap!

Usheen goes into the bathroom

Fintan (*examining the nightdress*) My God, she'd wear this for *him*, but I'm only let see her in her skin! It's so thin she must have paid a fortune for it. The faggot—spending my good money on clothes that are only meant to put on so as they can be ripped off. (*To Hoolihan*) Look at it. Jasus, what's wrong with flannelette? (*He throws it over Hoolihan's head*)

Usheen comes hopping out of the bathroom, happily removing his trousers. Humming a snatch of "Does your Mother Come from Ireland?", he begins to fold them neatly

We'll wait here—she'll be back. (*He slumps down on the bed again, knocking the breath out of Grainne*)

Usheen What the hell am I doing? They're not *my* trousers. (*He opens the wardrobe door wide, rolls the trousers into a ball, throws them in and closes* *the door. He comes down, takes up the brandy bottle and the remaining glass and begins to pour himself a drink. Suddenly he realizes what he has seen in the wardrobe. The neck of the bottle beats a frenzied tattoo against the lip of the glass. Almost in a whisper)* Grainne? Grainne, there's a corpse in the wardrobe.

The wardrobe door begins to creak open of its own accord. Usheen's nerve goes

(With a loud cry) Grainne!

Fintan leaps to his feet. Usheen grabs his overcoat and shoes and goes tearing out of the Emmet room and dashes off down the corridor

(As he goes) Grainne, where are you?
Fintan It came from outside. Follow me.
Hoolihan *(doing so)* Hup, two, three, four.
Fintan Shut up or I'll kill you.

Fintan and Hoolihan go into the Emmet room, just missing the sight of Usheen galloping down the corridor in his shorts. Fintan makes a quick reconnoitre, looking first into the bathroom. Grainne extricates herself from under the bed and goes cautiously into the corridor. In his lightning tour of the room, Fintan slams the wardrobe door shut

Someone's been in here. Look at this, a man's coat and tie, brandy and a shillelagh. This can only mean sex. Sit down, Hoolihan; they're gone now, but when they come back we'll be ready for them. Bring me that brandy.

Grainne, now at the door of the Emmet room, mouths the word "gone?" in puzzlement. She realizes that Usheen must be somewhere. She tiptoes along the passage

Grainne *(in a whispered shout)* Jay-ames, where are you? It's me-ee!

Grainne goes off up stage

(Softly) Woo-ooo?

Fintan and Hoolihan sit on the bed. A silence, broken only by Fintan thudding the shillelagh into his hand. On the fourth thud the shillelagh breaks neatly in two. He looks at it. There is a pause

Fintan Effin' Japanese shillelaghs. *(He helps himself to Usheen's brandy)*

The door of the wardrobe opens and Niamh crawls out, bent double. She practically walks into Hoolihan, who is looking at her. He salutes her. She returns the salute, turns and goes back into the wardrobe, closing the door

Hoolihan *(after a pause; conversationally)* Them is grand spacious wardrobes, sir.

Fintan grunts

I was up here in nineteen-sixteen. No motor car hotels up here then. No houses up here then. Nothing up here then, except me. Shot through the lung.

Fintan looks at him

Couldn't see the city with the smoke from the fires. Can't see it now with the rain.

Fintan You were shot?

Hoolihan "Is it rainin'?" some gobshite says to me in the South Dublin Union. So I look through the winda. Out in the yard there's a shagger in a tin helmet pointin' a gun at me. I seen the flash, but I didn't hear the bang. They say you don't, on account of the bullet gets to you before the bang does, and once the bullet gets to you you're not interested in listenin'. So I sit down on the floor. "Is it rainin'?" says the same gobshite to me. "No," says I, "but I am." Wasn't I quick, but?

Fintan How did you get up the mountains?

Hoolihan Yis.

Fintan I said how did you . . .

Hoolihan So they brung me up the mountains. This Volunteer puts me lyin' in the field and goes off to look for milk. Never cem back. "The sunlight'll do you good," he says. I have a bad chest ever since. He was another gobshite.

Fintan I'd offer you a drink, but there's only one glass.

Hoolihan unscrews the lens cap from his flashlight. He holds it out, and Fintan pours brandy into it

Hoolihan The brother got shot in nineteen-twenty, shot in the ankle. They gev him a pension, only he was in a motor-bike accident in nineteen-thirty-six and he lost his leg. The ankle went with it, so they stopped the pension. (*He drinks*) Thanks. Good job I didn't lose the lung. I do like walkin' around this wing, and I do like bein' in the restaurant with the big paintin's on the wall . . .

Fintan (*with pride*) The Famine room—best steaks in Ireland.

Hoolihan But I don't like the nineteen-sixteen wing. I don't like real things. But wasn't Mr Pearse full of ou' codology, wha'?

Fintan, his glass half-raised, stares at him

The rubbidge he used to come out with. "Never tell a lie. Strength in our hands, truth on our lips, and cleanness in our hearts." Jasus, what sort of way is that to run a country?

Fintan Nice talk from a man who fought in nineteen-sixteen!

Hoolihan Yous lot has more sense. I do like to see the big motor cars and the women with all the rings, and to feel the heat comin' out of the doors of the hotels. I do like to see everybody buyin' things and batin' the lard out of the other fella. Money is great, though.

Fintan How dare you criticize Pearse to me? You don't deserve to have been shot in the lung.

Hoolihan Decent man. "Freedom!" says he. They wouldn't have shot him
if they'd a known what we were goin' to do with it when he got it for us.
They were gobshites, too.

Fintan You ought to be ashamed of . . .

Hoolihan (*with dignity*) I have to go to the lav now. If I hadda had brains,
I'd be rich too, because it's the best nationality.

Hoolihan goes into the bathroom

Fintan follows him and stands in the doorway

Fintan You wouldn't be in the cushy job you're in today if it wasn't for
men like Pearse, Emmet and me. You're in a free country, and all you
can think of is money. And that carpet is new, and you're splashing it!
(*He comes back into the room in disgust and sits on the bed*)

*Miss Manning appears in the corridor upstage, followed by Dermod. She
comes down to the Parnell room*

Dermod Miss Manning, you don't have to inspect every room in the
building.

Miss Manning But I do, it's my job. Besides, my quarters, as charming as
they are, really do quite reek of paint . . .

Dermod I'm sorry about that . . .

Miss Manning So we must find me another little nest, hmm? Who is in
this room?

Dermod Parnell.

She waits for him to open the door. He does so. She goes in

Miss Manning 'nk yow!

Dermod The rooms are really all the same.

Miss Manning This one isn't. I spy with my little eye something beginning
with "n".

Dermod "N"?

Miss Manning (*holding up Grainne's nightdress*) For night attire.

Dermod How did that get there?

Miss Manning Oh, innocent Amy. As if you didn't know!

Dermod I don't.

Miss Manning You mean you haven't been entertaining young ladies here
on the sly?

Dermod Miss Manning, what an idea!

Miss Manning Yes, isn't it! (*Examining the nightdress*) I call this quite
saucy.

Dermod If that night watchman has been letting couples in here for
immoral purposes, I'll kick him the length of the building. That's
funny . . .

Miss Manning What is?

Dermod I—once bought my wife a nightdress like this.

Miss Manning Silly man. Of course she didn't wear it.

Dermod How do you know?

Miss Manning Wives never do. They can't bear the disappointed look on a man's face when he realizes that underneath the mint sauce is the same old mutton. (*She coughs modestly*)

Dermod (*stiffly*) As it happens, Miss Manning, my wife is an attractive woman.

Miss Manning Saddle of lamb? How nice.

Dermod And the nightdress was accidentally set fire to.

Miss Manning You were there?

Dermod She showed me the ashes.

Miss Manning (*drily*) There's no fooling you, is there, Mr Gibbon?

Dermod So if this room is to your liking . . .

Miss Manning I'm not sure. (*Pointing to the portrait*) Who is he?

Dermod Charles Stewart Parnell. My partner didn't want a room named after him, but we ran short of patriots. He destroyed himself because of a woman—an English woman.

Miss Manning This room will do nicely.

Dermod Good. I'll get your suitcase from reception.

Miss Manning It's been such a day. I can't face the thought of unpacking. And all my pretties are at the bottom.

Dermod Oh, yes?

Miss Manning Of my suitcase, Mr Gibbon. (*Holding the nightdress*) I know—why don't I wear this?

Dermod That?

Miss Manning Finders keepers, losers weepers. And as you can see, I'm the kind of woman who will wear any old thing. Let's hope this one won't go on fire.

Dermod Why, do you smoke in bed?

Miss Manning I was thinking of spontaneous combustion. Mr Gibbon, would you be so kind as to fetch me my little vanity case . . .

Dermod Certainly.

Miss Manning And then I hope you won't be in a hurry to be off.

Dermod Well, I . . .

Miss Manning (*reclining on the bed*) Because it's lonelier here than I had imagined. Also, there is such a thing as loneliness of the soul. Did I mention that my gentleman friend has left me?

Dermod I'm sorry to hear it.

Miss Manning 'nk yow! It happened after the party—the night you and I met. Mr Gibbon, you see before you a woman scorned. I gave that man the best nights of my life—and of his, too—and he threw me aside like an old bedsock. In my bitterness—(*all in one breath*)—I even thought of yielding my body to the first man with whom I should happen to find myself alone in a bedroom in a deserted building on a mountainside at dead of night, but of course that would have been silly. (*She looks at him inquiringly*)

Dermod (*his voice trembling*) Not necessarily.

Miss Manning (*kneeling up on the bed*) No? Mr Gibbon, I hope you're not about to make an erotic proposal.

Dermod (*retreating*) I wasn't.

Miss Manning I mean, just because we happen to be alone in a bedroom in a deserted building on a mountain-side at dead of night . . .
Dermod Are we?
Miss Manning Aren't we?
Dermod (*hoarsely*) Yes.
Miss Manning (*seizing him*) So kindly don't come any closer.
Dermod I won't.
Miss Manning (*pulling him on to the bed*) You aren't listening, are you? I mean it—not another step. (*She is now as close to him as she can get. She puts her arms around him, as if on the point of fainting*) There now. I knew I shouldn't be safe with you. Mr Gibbon, this is madness. Think what Mrs Gibbon would say——
Dermod I am.
Miss Manning —if you were silly enough to tell her.

Dermod attempts to return her embrace. At once she breaks away

(*Firmly*) No, it's too soon. The wounds go too deep. I shall need time.
Dermod (*crestfallen*) Of course.
Miss Manning Five minutes?
Dermod I'll get your vanity case.

Dermod goes out and hurries off up stage towards Reception

Miss Manning heads for the bathroom. On the way she sees the fur coat, which is on the floor where Fintan dropped it and has hitherto been hidden by the bed. She picks it up

Miss Manning (*casually*) Oh—nice. (*Carrying it into the bathroom*) James Usheen, I will be revenged on you this night!

Miss Manning goes off.
Hoolihan emerges from the bathroom

Hoolihan I enjoyed that.
Fintan You've been in there long enough to float a rowboat. In future use the staff lavatory down the hill.
Hoolihan Yis. (*He starts out*)
Fintan Not now, you've just been. Listen to me. I want you to go to the souvenir shop. (*Carefully, gripping Hoolihan by the lapels*) Get me another shillelagh. One that won't break. Do it now.
Hoolihan (*saluting Emmet*) Gone—all of them gone.
Fintan I said get out. And remember about that lavatory. I didn't lay out ten quid for corrugated iron for my own amusement.

Hoolihan goes out
Grainne appears from down stage with Usheen, still trouser-less, in tow

Grainne Dead women in wardrobes—I never heard such nonsense.

Usheen I tell you she . . .
Grainne Quiet! (*She starts violently as she comes face to face with Hoolihan*) Oh. (*Standing in front of Usheen*) Hello, we were just . . .
Hoolihan Gone.
Grainne Pardon me?
Hoolihan All gone now.
Grainne Do you mean that the gentleman who . . .
Hoolihan (*rubbing a window in the downstage "wall"*) How does water soak through glass? You don't know? (*Going*) He's another gobshite.

Hoolihan goes off

Grainne (*to Usheen*) Did you hear what he said? Fintan is gone. I'll just make sure. Shhh . . . (*She tiptoes to the door of the Emmet room*)

Inside the room, Fintan suddenly stands up

Fintan Shag him. Now he has *me* wanting to pee.
Usheen I refuse to set foot in that . . .

Fintan goes to the bathroom

Grainne motions Usheen to be silent, puts her ear to the door, then opens it cautiously just as Fintan disappears into the bathroom. She looks into the room, then turns to Usheen

Grainne We're safe. He's gone.
Usheen I'm not going in there. I tell you there was a dead woman in the wardrobe. She was huddled on the floor, a shapeless lump—her eyes were turned up. It was horrible. Funny thing is, she looked familiar.
Grainne (*nastily*) Are you sure she didn't have a mole on her breast?
Usheen If you're going to be rude I'll go home.
Grainne I'll tell you your trouble. You've been watching too much television.
Usheen I never watch television. I still have my pride.
Grainne What you don't have is your trousers, and they're in the wardrobe.
Usheen (*craven*) You get them.
Grainne First I have a question. Out of common Christianity, I offered to commit adultery with you tonight. Now—yes or no, James. Has rain stopped play?
Usheen I knew there was something I was trying to remember from twelve years ago. You're insane.
Grainne Thank you.
Usheen Have you forgotten? Your husband's partner is on the premises.
Grainne He'll have gone home by now. And it was Niamh he was after, not me—I can't think why. Luckily for her, she's miles away.

Niamh comes crawling out of the wardrobe again. She grabs the bedclothes and hoists herself on to her knees

So are we or aren't we?

Usheen I know you'll think me hypersensitive, but with a corpse under the same roof I doubt if my performance would be at its peak.

Grainne (*icily*) Very well, James, there's no more to be said. I'll get your trousers—my husband's trousers. Would you kindly fetch my nightie and mink—they're in there. (*She half opens the door of the Emmet room*)

Niamh (*seeing the door opening*) Oh, shag. (*She wearily returns into the wardrobe*)

Grainne And, James—don't blame me if wherever you go from now on you keep seeing your precious Lucretia. (*She goes into the Emmet room, shutting the door, and stands trying to fight back tears of fury*)

Usheen (*to the closed door*) Her name is Venetia. And I do not suffer from hallucinations.

Miss Manning comes in from the bathroom of the Parnell room dressed in the nightdress and mink coat

Usheen opens the door of the Parnell room just as Miss Manning enters it from the bathroom. They see each other and scream. Usheen slams the door shut

Miss Manning \
Usheen } Oh, my God.

Grainne hurries out

Grainne Now what? (*Looking at Usheen's stricken face*) What is it?

Usheen Forgive me. You were right and I was wrong. It's all in my mind. I'll do anything you say, only cure me, I'm sick. Where's the bed? (*He pushes past her into the bedroom*)

Grainne But what's happened?

Usheen I'm losing my sanity and she asks stupid questions. Are you coming to bed or aren't you?

Grainne I'll get my nightie. (*She stands for a moment, confused by this change of mind*)

Miss Manning is still reeling from shock in the Parnell room

Miss Manning I shall never eat British Rail mushrooms again.

Miss Manning goes into the bathroom

Grainne enters the Parnell room. Usheen, in the Emmet room, picks up his jacket and tie from the bed. He goes with them to the wardrobe and opens it

Niamh (*from within*) Hello, Mr Usheen.

Usheen looks at her blankly, then writes her off as an hallucination. He makes a dismissive gesture, hangs his jacket over her head, and closes the door. He gets into bed. Grainne cannot find her nightdress. She attempts to enter the bathroom but is surprised to find that the door is bolted

Miss Manning (*off*) Be patient, you impetuous man. I'll be out in a minute. And I've had rather a nasty shock, so you will be gentle with me, won't you, Mr Gibbon?

Grainne, facing down stage, is rigid with shock. She looks towards the audience and mouths "Mr Gibbon?". In the Emmet room, Usheen moves over in the bed so that there is space for Grainne. He plumps up her pillow. There is the sound of the toilet being flushed. Usheen looks towards the bathroom door, puzzled

Fintan comes out, drying his hands. He nods to Usheen

Fintan Evening. (*He sits on the edge of the bed, his back to Usheen. Very slowly, he realizes that the bed has an occupant. He stares at us with the same disbelief as is manifested by Grainne in the other room. Emitting a low animal growl, he turns slowly and points at Usheen*) Uhhh—hhh— hhh . . .

Usheen (*clutching the bedclothes around him*) I'm the first of the English visitors.

Fintan advances on him. Usheen gets out of bed on the far side

Is there anything I can do for you? Cup of sugar?

Fintan (*in a terrible voice*) Where is she?

Usheen She?

Fintan My adulterous trollop of a wife!

Usheen (*avoiding him*) I don't think I know the lady, but if I see anyone answering that description I'll . . .

Fintan Whoremaster!

Usheen Who came in?

Fintan Tell me where she is, and I'll give you the mercy of a swift death.

Usheen Keep away from me. I don't know where she is or . . .

Fintan Stop! I know your face.

Usheen (*seeing a way to safety*) Yes, most people do. And when you realize who I am, I think you'll change your tune, my man.

Fintan Wait—I know who you are!

Usheen I thought it would come to you.

Fintan You're Lester Piggott.

Usheen Try again.

Fintan Where was it? Where did I see you?

Usheen (*confident now*) I presume you watch television?

A wild, drawn-out shriek from Fintan

Oh, God, an Andrews fan.

Fintan You! The atheist, the adulterer. And my wife says she's mad about you.

Usheen Everybody is—don't take it personally.

Hoolihan appears in the corridor at a senile jogtrot, carrying another shillelagh

Meanwhile Grainne is now pacing up and down the Parnell room like a tigress waiting for mealtime

Usheen Sir, if any harm comes to me, I have twelve million devoted fans who will . . .

As Fintan raises his hands as if in prayer. Hoolihan enters behind him and slides the shillelagh into his fist. Fintan makes a gesture of thanks towards heaven

Fintan A time-honoured Irish weapon!
Usheen (*wearily*) Why did I ever come back?
Fintan *Now!* (*He raises the shillelagh on high. This one does not break. Instead, it droops like a withered flower*)

All three men look at it

Never mind. I'll kill him with my bare hands. And no-one will hear your screams—there's not a soul within five miles.

Dermod appears in the corridor, singing loudly to himself and carrying Miss Manning's vanity case

Dermod (*singing*) "There's a small motel,
               And a wishing well,
               I wish that we were there
               Togeth-er . . ."

Fintan and Grainne both react in their respective rooms. Fintan goes to the door in time to see Dermod entering the Parnell room. Grainne, hearing him approaching, stands against the wall so that the opening door will conceal her

(*Entering*) I'm ba-ack!

At once, Miss Manning appears from the bathroom, every inch the man-eater in mink and nylon

Miss Manning (*archly*) Well, Mr Gibbon?
Dermod (*stunned*) Miss Manning, you're . . .
Miss Manning I'm what?
Dermod You're beautiful.
Miss Manning (*modestly*) You're blind.
Grainne (*appearing from behind the door*) You're banjaxed!
Dermod (*thunderstruck*) Grainne . . .
Grainne Who is this faggot?
Miss Manning Oh, very nice.
Dermod Now, don't jump to conclusions . . .
Grainne I know—you can explain everything! You, the man I trusted. I turn my back on you for an evening, and I find you here with that . . .
Usheen (*from the other room*) Grainne, save me!

Grainne Alone in a bedroom with that woman wearing my . . .
Dermod Who was that?
Grainne (*smiling brightly*) No-one, dear. (*Resuming her tirade*) Wearing my fur coat and my—my . . .
Usheen (*yelling*) Grainne!
Dermod No-one, eh? Well, let's see what no-one looks like! (*He marches out and into the Emmet room*)

Grainne, now frantic, follows him

Grainne Wait—I can explain everything.

Dermod comes face to face with Fintan. Grainne comes in. Miss Manning straggles after them as far as the doorway

Dermod (*to Fintan*) What are you doing here? (*He sees Usheen*) And who is he?
Grainne I never saw him before.
Dermod (*taking a closer look*) It's Mr Usheen.
Usheen Hello. Lovely to see you again.
Miss Manning It *wasn't* the mushrooms!
Dermod (*with hand outstretched*) Forgive me, I didn't recognize you with your . . . (*He takes in Usheen's state of undress*) You! You and my . . .
Grainne Now don't jump to conclusions.
Dermod Him—the man you said you can't stand . . .
Usheen (*to Grainne*) Did you say that?
Dermod Yes—now I see it all.
Grainne Never mind what *you* see. (*Pointing at Miss Manning*) What about what *I* see?
Usheen What about what *I* see?
Fintan Yes, who the hell is that?
Miss Manning (*explaining everything*) I'm the new manageress.
Hoolihan Hih-hih-hih-hih!
Dermod ⎫
Fintan ⎬ Shut up!
Fintan My God—you and her and her and him. Orgies under the Plough and the Stars—the Patrick Pearse Motel turned into a knocking shop. What sort of savages am I living with? And me—I'm the worst of the lot. I thought bad of the only decent, pure, honest woman left in the country. Niamh, Niamh—say you forgive me!
Niamh (*coming out of the wardrobe*) I do!—I do!

Fintan looks at her and screams. The Lights black-out and—

the CURTAIN *falls*

SCENE 2

The same. Five minutes have passed

When the Curtain rises, Dermod, Grainne and Usheen—still without his trousers—are sitting on what transpires to be Fintan spreadeagled on the bed. Hoolihan is sitting on the floor in a corner of the room with the brandy bottle, from which he helps himself during the scene. Niamh is standing as far away from Fintan as she can get

There is a pause, then Miss Manning comes out of the bathroom in the Parnell room. She is dressed as in the previous scene. She picks up her vanity case and returns to the bathroom

Grainne We can't go sitting on him all night.

Usheen If we get off now he'll go berserk again.

Dermod He's been quiet for a while now. Should we chance it?

Niamh Don't. He's the same at home; not a stir out of him in bed, and when you think he's asleep, that's when he turns into a madman.

Dermod We've got to let him up some time. (*He lifts the pillow which he has been holding over Fintan's head*) Fintan, are you all right?

Fintan (*gasping*) Get off me.

Dermod If we do, will you promise to be good? No more trying to strangle Niamh?

Niamh If you're going to let him up, at least give me a ten-minute head-start.

Dermod Fintan, we want your word that you'll behave.

Fintan (*hoarsely*) Yes.

Dermod You swear as a gentleman?

Fintan I swear as a gentleman.

Niamh (*hollowly*) Oh, Jay.

Dermod All right. (*To Grainne and Usheen*) Slowly now . . .

They get up as gingerly as if they were sitting on nitro-glycerine. Fintan arises like a whale surfacing. He bestows a baleful glance upon Niamh

Niamh Watch him!

Fintan (*with massive dignity*) I intend to prosecute everyone here for assault and being sat down on. (*Indicating Usheen*) I intend to sue *him* for enticement and loss of a housekeeper. (*Indicating Niamh*) As for her, I intend to get a Papal annulment. You'll be hearing from my bishop in the morning.

Niamh And now for the *bad* news!

Dermod She won't be the only one who'll be hearing from a bishop.

Grainne Meaning me?

Dermod (*addressing the ceiling*) I'd say the Vatican is in for a profitable year.

Usheen That'll be a change!

Dermod glares at him

I suppose we should be thankful he doesn't intend to have us up for G.B.H.

Fintan What's G.B.H.?

Dermod It stands for Grainne Being Had.

Grainne How dare you? You can accuse me after I saw you with that sex-mad rip wearing my—(*amending*)—wearing a disgusting see-through nightdress.

Usheen That's unfair. Venetia is definitely not sex-mad. I've known her to go without it for hours on end.

Dermod At least Miss Manning was here by right. She's the manageress.

Grainne She certainly goes in for room service in a big way.

Usheen That's not bad.

Dermod (*pointing at Usheen*) Does *he* belong here? Look at him. He's in his underwear.

Fintan (*scowling*) Pansy.

Usheen There's a very simple explanation for that . . .

Fintan ⎫
Dermod ⎭ Yes?

Usheen (*to Grainne*) Tell them.

Grainne Certainly. Niamh, tell them.

Niamh Me? (*Taking a deep breath*) Well, when a ship is launched, it's always the owner's wife who . . .

Graine (*panic-stricken*) Don't listen to her. If you want the truth, James couldn't find a hotel room in town, so I brought him here.

Dermod You're lying.

Grainne Ask James.

Usheen Ask me.

Grainne James and I were good friends once. What more natural than that he should ring up and ask if I knew of a place where he could stay?

Dermod (*almost convinced*) I see.

Grainne And Niamh came along as my chaperone. You know how people talk.

Fintan (*to Niamh*) Is this true?

Niamh May I drop down dead.

Dermod (*to Fintan*) It sounds plausible.

Grainne Do I offer him a room in our house, with you away? No, I bring him here, seven miles up a mountain road. I try to protect my good name, and this is the thanks I get.

Dermod (*now contrite*) Grainne, I . . .

Usheen (*heading for the door*) Well, now that that's cleared up . . .

Fintan Where are you going?

Usheen Back to my hotel. (*He comes to a shuddering standstill*)

Fintan ⎫
Dermod ⎭ (*to Niamh and Grainne respectively*) Liar!

Usheen No, no, what I mean is to *look* for a ho . . .

Dermod (*coldly*) The best thing you can do at the moment is to put your trousers on.

Fintan Yes, there are whores present.

Grainne (*to Fintan*) Are you calling me a . . .

Niamh Don't contradict him, it puts him in a bad humour.

Grainne (*to Dermod*) Are you going to let him insult your wife?

Dermod turns his back on her

I swear on my mother's grave I'm innocent.

Dermod Your mother's alive.

Grainne (*snapping*) Her grave is paid for.

Dermod (*losing his temper*) By me, more fool that I am. And may she never live to climb into it.

Grainne That's it, now abuse my mother, a woman in constant pain.

Dermod She's worse than in constant pain, she's in a council house in Crumlin.

Grainne How dare you throw Crumlin in my face, with your own parents slobbering in the shadow of a brewery? And if my mother's in Crumlin, *who left her there to rot?*

Usheen takes his (Dermod's) trousers from the wardrobe and puts them on, having trouble with the zip

Dermod I wish I'd left more than your mother to rot in Crumlin. I wish I'd . . . (*He laughs derisively at Usheen's trouble with the zip*) Ha! Ha-ha!

Grainne What?

Dermod Your fancy-man's taste in trousers is well in keeping with his taste in women. Yech!

Grainne emits a loud, shrill laugh

What's so funny?

Grainne I'll tell you after the annulment.

Usheen (*struggling with the zip*) Bugger it! Excuse me . . .

Niamh Can I help you with your fly, Mr Usheen?

An anguished growl from Fintan

Now what?

Fintan (*starting forward*) I'll kill her, I'll kill her!

Dermod Fintan, you promised . . .

Fintan (*picking up an easy chair*) Only not to strangle her.

Niamh I only offered to . . .

Fintan I know what you were offering to do for him, I've seen you in action. You didn't learn that at your Oratorio practice.

Niamh Learn what?

Fintan I curse that hour and a half we spent in the airport in Paris on our way back from Lourdes.

Niamh (*to the others; reasonably*) His own mother told me not to marry him.

Usheen (*who has been thinking*) "I'll kill her, I'll kill her!"

The others look at him

    (*To Fintan*) I know where I've seen you before. The bastard in the Jensen.

Fintan The what in the what?

Usheen That face, that voice. Sir, allow me to inform you that you are without doubt the most wantonly irresponsible driver since Ben Hur. Where did you learn to drive, anyway—reform school? Do you know I could have you prosecuted?

Fintan First he depraves my wife, now he criticizes my driving. Get him out of here.

Dermod (*to Usheen*) You'd better go.

Usheen points a denunciatory finger at Fintan. This involves his letting go of his trousers, which fall down. He picks them up, turning his attention to Dermod

Usheen (*to Dermod*) You were in the car with him, weren't you? In which case, you can whistle for your trousers. And furthermore . . . ! (*He kisses Niamh, then goes out and into the Parnell room*)

Fintan roars with rage

Dermod I wouldn't be seen dead in those . . . (*Staring at Grainne*) He's wearing my . . .

Grainne His got wet.

Dermod You gave him my good fifteen-guinea . . .

Niamh She had to.

Dermod *Had* to?

Niamh Fintan nearly ran over him. (*To Fintan*) What if he does go to the police?

Fintan I can't be prosecuted. I'm out of that income group.

Dermod (*to Grainne*) You gave him my . . .

Grainne Oh, shut up. And before you start throwing more sand in my eyes about your trousers, my semi-invalid mother and James Usheen, let me remind you that *I* was not the person who was caught red-handed with a nymphomaniac wearing a nightdress you could see the Hell-Fire Club through.

Dermod Yes, *about* that nightdress . . . !

Grainne (*knowing what is coming*) Don't change the subject.

Dermod When Miss Manning walked into that room, the nightdress was already there. So where did it come from?

Grainne How do I know where it . . .

Dermod It was yours.

Grainne Mine?

Dermod I bought it for you.

Fintan For *her?* (*With an incredulous laugh*) You madman.

Grainne That nightdress was set fire to.

Dermod So you said. I remember I bought it at Chez Siobhan's. Why don't I go and get it, and we'll have a look at the label?

Grainne and Niamh look at each other in horror. Dermod starts towards the door

Good idea, yes?
Fintan (*magisterially*) Wait just one minute!

In the Parnell room, Usheen taps on the door of the bathroom

Usheen Venetia? My zip is stuck.
Miss Manning (*off*) I don't give a fig. Kindly go away.
Dermod (*to Fintan*) Well?
Fintan Man, are you so blind that you can't see the truth? That nightdress isn't hers . . .
Grainne Of course it isn't.
Fintan (*indicating Niamh*) It's *hers*, and your wife is protecting her. Look at those two women, compare them. Now to hell with loyalty, own up. If you were a dirty anglicized renegade Irishman looking for his oats, which one of them would you go to bed with?
Niamh He's off.

Dermod looks dumbly at Fintan

Fintan I see by your face you agree with me. But don't think your wife is innocent. The ugly ones always encourage the good-looking ones.
Grainne (*indignantly*) I beg your p . . .
Fintan (*to Niamh; brokenly*) How could you do it to me? Have I ever neglected you?
Niamh No, not once.
Fintan Was the sight of me raking in money not happiness enough for you? And if you had to commit adultery, why did you disgrace me by choosing *him*? Why couldn't you have picked a decent, good-living Catholic? Why? Why? (*He kneels before her*)
Niamh (*stroking his head; kindly*) I will, next time.
Fintan A man who gets on the television and belittles us in colour. He was the one who said that the Irish are under the influence of L.S.D.— laziness, slander and dirt. How dare he say that we're lazy? I'll get up early one of these days and kill him for that. (*Still on his knees, he "walks" to the door and shouts, for Usheen's benefit*) What's more, I'm going to sue him and expose him!
Usheen Ventia, he says he's going to sue me and expose me.

Miss Manning comes out of the bathroom, now dressed. She gets ready to leave

Miss Manning High time, too.
Dermod Fintan, get up. (*He attempts to help Fintan*)
Fintan Get your hands off me! You're as bad as they are—the first member of the staff to arrive, and you have her in her pelt before she has time to count the towels. You don't fool me.
Grainne Nor me.

Dermod Fintan, I want a private word with you.

Fintan I have nothing to say to any of you.

Dermod This is about money.

Fintan I couldn't care less.

Dermod A lot of money.

Fintan I said I don't want to talk to you.

Dermod (*curtly*) Very well.

Fintan But if you're going to nag at me, I'll listen.

Dermod If the ladies would excuse us . . . ?

Grainne Leave you? With pleasure. Excuse you? Not if you were to come
  begging on your hands and knees, and wearing a see-through nightdress! Come, Niamh, now that we're free women again, we have plans
  to make.

Niamh (*following her*) Oh, Jay.

Grainne and Niamh go into the bathroom and shut the door

Dermod goes to the door and listens

Fintan I'm done with you.

Dermod Shhh!

Fintan Don't you tell me to shush. Thanks to you, my marriage is in
  flitters, the motel is a mockery, and the cost of the Papal annulment will
  put me in the poorhouse.

Dermod (*impatiently*) Will you wait . . . (*He listens*)

In the Parnell room, Miss Manning is ready to be off

Usheen Venetia, where are you going?

Miss Manning Kensington High Street.

Usheen Good, I'll go with you.

Miss Manning I'll feel safer on my own—'nk yow!

Usheen You silly cow, you'll drown in a boghole. Don't you know that
  it's pouring with rain and you're on top of a mountain?

Miss Manning Kindly move to one side.

Usheen At least help me get this fastened.

Miss Manning I've pulled up your last zip, James. And now I intend to
  give myself to the first gentleman farmer I meet on my way down the
  mountain.

Usheen If this is because of what happened tonight, I'm as innocent as
  you are.

Miss Manning How do you know I'm innocent?

Usheen Because this bloody country hasn't changed. They can't even
  commit adultery properly. Venetia, don't leave me alone with the one
  they call Fintan.

Miss Manning I won't say good-bye, James. You said it in London when
  you sent me out to buy my trousseau, and then changed the locks.

Miss Manning goes off, heading towards Reception

Usheen Venetia, wait. (*To his zip*) Come up, come up . . .

In the Emmet room, Dermod comes away from the door of the bathroom

Dermod I knew it. They're trying to think up a good story.
Usheen (*in triumph*) Got it!
Dermod Grainne is asking Niamh to . . .

Usheen emits a scream of agony. He doubles up, his arms folded across his thighs. The pain continues

Usheen Aaaaah . . .
Dermod My God, what was that?
Fintan Hah! The decent man has cut his throat.

Usheen, still bent double, stumbles across the corridor and into the Emmet room. He stares at Dermod and Fintan, too agonized to speak

Usheen Aaaaah . . .
Dermod What do you want?
Usheen (*begging for help*) Aaaaah . . .
Dermod That's a bloody funny place to cut your throat.
Fintan Go away, we're not talking to you.

Usheen utters another "Aaaaah . . ." and staggers across the room and into the bathroom

Where's he going? Come back here!

There are loud screams from Grainne and Niamh off

Usheen is thrown out of the bathroom. His first loud cry has brought Miss Manning hurrying back along the corridor. Grainne and Niamh reappear

Grainne Filthy beast.
Niamh But thanks for the compliment.

Niamh and Grainne return to the bathroom and close the door

Usheen is as much in agony as ever. Miss Manning looks into the Parnell room

Dermod You! Did you attack my wife?
Fintan Of course he did. The state he's in, he'd attack any old thing.
    Look at him—that's what television does.
Dermod (*advancing on Usheen*) You animal. But God, I'll . . .
Miss Manning (*coming in*) James!
Usheen (*seeing her*) Aaaaah . . .
Miss Manning Are you ill?
Usheen (*negative*) Aaaaah . . .
Miss Manning Is it your zip?
Usheen (*affirmative*) Aaaaah . . .

Miss Manning (*to the others*) I'm afraid he's done himself a little mischief. Come with Venetia, dear. (*She takes Usheen and leads him, still bent double, into the Parnell room and towards the bathroom*)

On the way, Usheen attempts to speak to her

Usheen Aaah . . . aaah . . . aaah.
Miss Manning I know, pet. That's why I'm glad I'm a girl.

Miss Manning and Usheen go into the bathroom

Fintan stares after them from the Emmet room. Dermod gets down to business

Dermod Fintan, we must make it up with the girls.
Fintan To hell with them.
Dermod And with each other.
Fintan Get stitched.
Dermod If we don't make it up, there'll be a scandal.
Fintan Damn sure there'll be a scandal. If I've got to be the innocent party, I'll have something to show for it. I'll spread these goings-on all over town like jam on bread.
Dermod Right. Then you can say good-bye to the motel.
Fintan Don't threaten me, you pup.
Dermod Fintan, this is no ordinary enterprise. (*Mistily*) Our motel is the fulfilment of the dreams of the men who died for this green island. Do you want to insult their memory? Do you want to make their deaths meaningless? Do you want us to go bankrupt?
Fintan (*grabbing him*) You know something—tell me.
Dermod I'm telling you that if there is one whisper of scandal there'll be no grand opening next week. Think of it, Fintan. No cabinet minister to unveil the bust in the De Valera Snackery, no bishop to bless our Kitchen Garden of Remembrance, no guard of honour to fire a salute over the swimming pool. Is that what you want?
Fintan Don't go on.
Dermod We may as well put a note in the brochure:, "Unmarried Couples Welcome—Fornicate in Comfort."
Fintan Stop, stop . . .
Dermod "Wine, Dine and Have It Away by Candlelight."
Fintan Stop, or I'll kill you.
Dermod If you won't think of us, think of the employment we're giving. What's going to happen to the staff who'll be depending on us?
Fintan They'll all have to go back to Cyprus.
Dermod Exactly. Our wives are in there now, going through hell to think up a tissue of lies. Fintan, what kind of men are we that we won't meet them half-way?
Fintan I'm a patriot: that means I'll believe anything.

Miss Manning and Usheen come out of the bathroom into the Parnell room. Usheen is visibly shaken after his experience

Miss Manning A little soreness won't harm you, James. None of this
would have happened if you'd married me.

Usheen I've already explained to you why I can't.

Miss Manning For religious reasons?

Usheen Yes.

Miss Manning What a bigot you are in this day and age. After all, it's the
the same God we all disbelieve in, isn't it?

Usheen There's another reason.

Miss Manning Might I know it?

Usheen I can't stand you.

Miss Manning You sillikins, that's not a reason. You've simply found out
before marriage what other husbands and wives find out afterwards.

Usheen Venetia, there are two men in there who are prepared to sue me
and cause a scandal.

Miss Manning They won't cause a scandal.

Usheen They're Irish-Catholic business men. They'd cut your head off and
charge you for corkage.

Miss Manning They won't cause a scandal, because I can stop them.

Usheen How?

Miss Manning If I did, would you marry me?

Usheen No.

Miss Manning Not ever?

Usheen (*firmly*) I'd sooner spend the rest of my life caught in a zip.

Miss Manning Oh. (*With a strange smile*) Never mind, perhaps I'll help
you all the same. (*Tapping his cheek*) I'm so fond of you.

Usheen (*facing front*) Why do I suddenly feel so frightened?

*Niamh and Grainne come from the bathroom. Grainne has a coolly defiant
look on her face; Niamh is downcast*

Fintan and Dermod rise expectantly

Fintan }
Dermod } (*with welcoming smiles*) Well?

Grainne Perfectly.

Niamh We're grand, thanks.

Dermod (*warmly*) What Fintan and I mean is, have you anything to tell
us?

The women look at him blankly

We know you were both innocent, don't we, Fintan?

Fintan (*non-committal*) Ugh.

Dermod We were just naturally wondering how you came to be up here
with him. Not that we're in the least bit suspicious.

Silence

Fintan (*appealingly*) Niamh?

Niamh When a ship is launched, it's always the . . .

Grainne (*silencing her*) Quiet, Niamh! (*To the men*) We have nothing to say.

Dermod Nothing?

Fintan Any old rubbish would do us.

Dermod Try us with anything.

Grainne (*turning on him*) All right then, you sarcastic devils. All right, if you want the truth, you can have it!

Fintan (*in dismay*) The truth?

Dermod Who said anything about the truth?

Fintan (*wheeling on Dermod*) Now look what you've done!

Grainne I *planned* to come up here with James Usheen. We were going to make . . .

Miss Manning is in the room with Usheen in her wake

Miss Manning . . . going to make this nice motel of yours famous! (*She goes straight to Grainne, as if they were long-lost sisters*) You poor thing—having to keep silent for James's sake and mine. But I've spoken to James, and it's not a secret any more. (*To Usheen*) Is it, dear?

Usheen looks at her, open-mouthed

Now we can let it be known what a brave, good wife you are. Shall I tell them, or will you?

Grainne and Niamh look at each other blankly, then at Miss Manning

Grainne
Niamh } You tell them.

Miss Manning Hem! (*Indicating Grainne*) This lady—may I call you Grainy?—wrote to Mr Usheen some weeks ago and asked if he would interview her husband and this charming gentleman—(*indicating Fintan*)—on his programme. To publicize the motel, you know.

Fintan Us? Him and me? On colour?

Dermod Grainne, is this true?

Grainne (*staring dazedly at Miss Manning*) Every word.

Miss Manning That was why Mr Usheen asked me to apply for the position of manageress. I haven't been honest with you, Mr Gibbon—I'm really here as a kind of spy—a snooper.

Niamh (*to Grainne*) She's very good.

Miss Manning Mind, what I've seen, I like. And to make doubly sure, Mr Usheen came up here this evening with Mrs Gibbon to inspect the premises for himself.

Usheen is oozing relief. He puts an arm around Miss Manning

Usheen And I can't tell you how impressed I am.

Fintan Stop right there—I believe everything.

Dermod Grainne, can you forgive me?

Grainne (*"wounded"*) Not if I live to be thirty.

Miss Manning Hem! Now you may ask, why should Mr Usheen and I visit the motel separately on the same night? Shall we tell them, Grainy?

Grainne (*being big about it*) Yes, why keep it to ourselves!

Miss Manning James?

Usheen (*squeezing her; lavishly*) Tell them everything!

Miss Manning I mean to. You might say that James and I are combining business with pleasure. After all, what better place than this for a quiet honeymoon?

Usheen Absolutely. It's peaceful, it's secluded—it's a lie.

Miss Manning (*playfully*) Now you did say I could tell them. You're the first to know. James and I were married yesterday.

Usheen (*appalled*) Venetia, you b . . .

A peal of hysterical laughter from Grainne

Miss Manning We told Grainy, of course. As you can see, she's so happy for us.

Niamh Oh, Jay.

Grainne I think I'm going to choke.

Miss Manning So, as we're newly-weds, James would hardly be interested in another lady, now would he? Nor I in another gentleman. Although I did rather flirt with Mr Gibbon, just to keep him from suspecting.

Usheen (*feebly*) Look this is all a——

Miss Manning —a dead secret—until Sunday. That's when James is going to make it public on television. Aren't you, pet?

Usheen And if I don't?

Miss Manning Eamonn Andrews will.

Dermod (*bounding forward*) Mr Usheen—congratulations.

Fintan (*hand outstretched*) I was always a fan of yours. Put it there.

It is all too much for Usheen. His shoulders begin to heave

Miss Manning (*touched*) Ahhh—he's so sentimental deep down. (*She chucks him under the chin*) Yes, he—is!

Usheen You . . .

Usheen's hands begin to reach for Miss Manning's throat, but Fintan wraps a massive arm around his shoulder

Fintan Come here to me, me old son. You won't forget about putting us on TV?

Miss Manning I'll remind him.

Fintan And you'll give us the full treatment? I mean, the few little friendly insults?

Usheen looks at him. At once his rage finds an outlet

Usheen Yes! Yes, just to begin with, I think I'll call you an overstuffed upstart, who drives like a drunken Seminole Indian, and who combines the brains of a brontosaurus with the manners of a mongoose.

Fintan (*wildly*) I like it, I like it!

Miss Manning And now, who would like to kiss the bride? Mr Gibbon?

Dermod kisses her and is kissed back

'nk yow! (*She sees that Fintan is next in line*) Oh, I like them big. Jus a peck now! (*She leaves Fintan gasping*) 'nk *yow!* Well, now, who's next? Oh, no!

This is a reaction to the appearance of Hoolihan beside her. He has risen from the floor, and Miss Manning assumes that he wishes to kiss her

Hoolihan I only want to get past. I have to go to the lav. I have sudden kidneys.

Miss Manning stands back

Thanks. (*He heads for the bathroom*)
Fintan The outside lavatory!
Hoolihan Oh, yes.

Hoolihan goes out and off down stage

Fintan (*good-humouredly*) You should have given him a kiss. It'd probably have been his last.
Dermod Fintan, the day we appear on English television we'll be set up for life.
Grainne And all thanks to me.
Dermod No man ever had a better wife.
Fintan I told you all along the girls were innocent. Niamh, when we get home I'm going to make it up to you.
Niamh I think I'll slash my wrists.

They all come out in a group and move down stage, Fintan carrying the brandy bottle

Miss Manning Do try to smile, James. After all, marriage is only another form of entertainment tax.
Fintan Will you look at this? The old get drank the lot. (*He holds up the bottle*)
Dermod We should get rid of him.
Fintan I'll give him the boot first thing in the morning. (*To Usheen*) Now about this television lark . . .
Miss Manning Somebody's just gone past the window.
Dermod Where? (*He comes down stage and peers out*) It's Hoolihan. He's gone off up the mountain.
Fintan There's so much brandy in him he can't see straight.
Niamh (*to Fintan*) Maybe you ought to go after him.
Fintan Who, me?
Niamh It's as black as pitch out, and it's teeming.
Grainne (*not too concerned*) He's nearly eighty.
Dermod If he goes over that rise he won't even see the lights of the motel.
Usheen He could die of exposure.
Niamh Or the wind could blow him over or he could get pneumonia or fall into a . . .
Fintan Nag, nag, nag! If we go out there, we could all get lost. I want to talk to James about this interview. (*To Usheen*) Will we need dress suits?

Niamh (*upset*) Fintan!

Fintan All right! We'll give the old drunkard twenty minutes. If he's not back by then, I'll drive down to Foxrock, pick up a couple of flash-lamps, wellington boots and raincoats, and we'll go and look for him. Fair?

Dermod More than fair.

Niamh But by then he could be . . .

Fintan Don't spoil the evening for us. We won't see him stuck. He was out in nineteen-sixteen—he's one of us.

Fintan, Miss Manning, Usheen, Dermod and Niamh go off up stage, talking. The following is played very fast, with speeches overlapping

Now about our other motel in Cork—the Michael Collins . . .

Dermod Hey, we might accept an investment.

Usheen Really?

Fintan If you're interested.

Usheen I could get my hands on twenty thousand . . .

Fintan You're in!

Grainne disengages herself from Dermod's arm and comes down to us, again with her warm hostessy smile

Grainne Hello, again. Please don't think we're not worried about Mr— I forget his name—because we really are. So, as you can see, money hasn't spoiled us one bit. We're still very humanitarian. And Dermod and I do hope you'll drop in on us—at the motel, that is, not at the house. I'm afraid we have so many close friends. But—and we sincerely mean this—if you happen to be in town and you see our Jensen, do wave to us as you jump clear.

Grainne blows us a kiss, as—

the CURTAIN *falls*

FURNITURE AND PROPERTY LIST

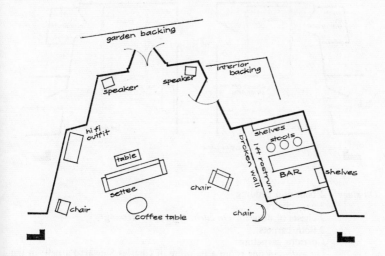

ACT I

On stage: Sofa
      Sofa table. *On it:* telephone, Grainne's handbag with spectacles.
        Niamh's handbag with letter in envelope and car keys
      Coffee-table
      2 armchairs
      Hifi system and 2 loud-speakers, with records
      Bar with 3 stools. *On shelves or under counter:* bottles of champagne,
        brandy, whisky, various glasses, dressing
      Carpet
      Window curtains
      On walls: paintings by Yeats, Keating and O'Sullivan

Off stage: Dermod's and Fintan's coats and scarves (**Grainne**)
      Dermod's trousers (**Grainne**)
      Hatchet (**Fintan**)
      Address book (**Niamh**)

Personal: **Fintan:** wristwatch
      Grainne: wristwatch, brooch, handkerchief

ACT II

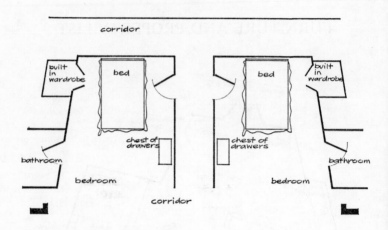

On stage: 2 beds and bedding
2 easy chairs
2 chests of drawers. *On each:* 2 glasses, dressing
2 floor carpets
Corridor carpeting
On walls: in one room a painting of Charles Stewart Parnell: in the
other a painting of Robert Emmet

Off stage: Breakable shillelagh (**Hoolihan**)
Pliable shillelagh (**Hoolihan**)
Brandy (**Grainne**)
Vanity case (**Dermod**)

Personal: **Grainne:** handbag with 2 toothbrushes, nylon nightdress
Hoolihan: flashlight

LIGHTING PLOT

ACT I

Property fittings required: small chandelier, wall-brackets
    Interior. A living-room

To open: Chandelier and brackets lit

No cues

ACT II

Property fittings required: 4 wall-brackets, corridor lights

SCENE 1

To open: All interior lighting on

Cue 1   **Niamh: "I do—I do."**   (Page 55)
             Black-out

SCENE 2

To open: As Scene 1

No cues

EFFECTS PLOT

ACT I

Cue 1   **On** CURTAIN up   (Page 1)
Demonstration disc on hifi

Cue 2   **Dermod** turns record off   (Page 1)
Disc off

Cue 3   **Grainne:** "Ssssh!"   (Page 12)
Sound of car driving away

Cue 4   **Grainne:** ". . . have one yourself."   (Page 13)
Sound of car arriving

Cue 5   **Grainne:** "Zip me up."   (Page 15)
Sound of car driving off

Cue 6   **Miss Manning** starts music   (Page 34)
Sensuous music

Cue 7   **Miss Manning** stops record player   (Page 34)
Music off

ACT II

SCENE 1

Cue 8   **Usheen** plumps up pillow   (Page 53)
Sound of toilet being flushed

SCENE 2

No cues

HUGH LEONARD

THE
PATRICK PEARSE
MOTEL

ISBN 0 573 01333 0

7207 W 2 7